SAN LUIS OBISPO COUNTY

Trail
Guide

A guide to over fifty public hiking trails
with new maps and trail descriptions

Completely revised and enlarged third edition

SIERRA
CLUB
Santa Lucia Chapter
Preserving California's Central Coast

Santa Lucia Chapter of the Sierra Club

San Luis Obispo, California

ISBN: 1-930401-07-8

Illustrations by Margaret Foster and Karen Foster-Wells.

Cover photo: Sierra Club volunteer Carlos Diaz-Saavedra on Castle Crags, Machesna Wilderness.

Cover Photo by Gary Felsman.

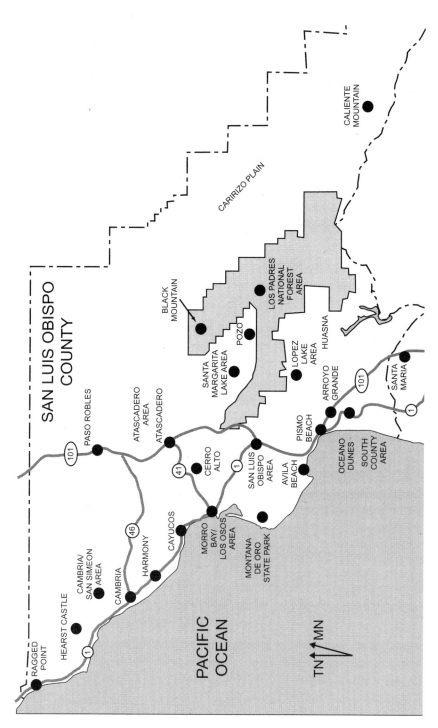

San Luis Obispo County

Contents

Index to Maps

Acknowledgments

This third edition of the Sierra Club Trail Guide is the result of hundreds of hours of dedicated service by Sierra Club members. Whether hiking the trails or working on the myriad tasks associated with creating a publication, volunteers gave freely of their time and talents. We would especially like to acknowledge the following:

Gary Felsman, who spearheaded the project. Over a period of three years, Gary and his wife Darlene hiked all the trails in this Guide. After each hike, the two wrote down a preliminary trail description.

The new maps represent literally hundreds of hours of work by Gary Felsman, with the help of Judy Lang.

Deborah Krueger coordinated the project and served as liaison with the Board.

Cameron Macgregor Clark and Monica Tarzier spent long hours at the computer to ready the Guide for publication.

Carlos Diaz-Saavedra, Betty Schetzer, Monica Tarzier and Rosemary Wilvert edited the book for clarity and accuracy.

Many hikers variously measured trails, critiqued the descriptions, and helped in various ways, including Willy Amarillas, Steve Boyer, Tess Deery, Carlos Diaz-Saavedra, Kathy Hawkins, Dorothy Krueger, Katie Krupp, Joanie LaVire, Holly Naylor, Al Normandin, Scott Reckefus, Bev Sessa, Shirley Sparling, Chuck Tribbey, Lisa Wallender, Jim Wilson, and Rosemary Wilvert.

The staff of Poor Richards Press helped with preliminary advice and support.

Finally, thanks go to Manny Madrigal of the US Forest Service, Santa Maria station, for cheerful cooperation and assistance.

About the Illustrations

The landscape illustrations found throughout this Guide are the work of Margaret Foster, art teacher, fashion illustrator, mural painter, and dedicated Sierra Club member for 25 years until her death in 1990. She played an active part in the creation of the first edition of this Trail Guide by helping map, measure, and name trails. She also led hikes on the trails she helped document. In order not to miss any chance to capture the beauty of the area, Margaret carried with her a pad of archival Bristol paper and a small army-surplus ammunition box with dip pens and bottles of ink.

Margaret was not the only artist in the family. We owe the beautiful drawings of animals to her daughter, Karen Foster-Wells.

SURF AT SPOONERS COVE   MONTANA DE ORO

About the Sierra Club

The Sierra Club is an international environmental organization founded in California over a century ago. Its presence in this state continues to be strong: one-third of its nationwide membership comes from California. The Santa Lucia Chapter, chartered in 1968, includes nearly 2,000 members in San Luis Obispo County.

The Sierra Club promotes activities to explore, enjoy, and preserve the nation's forests, waters, wildlife, and wilderness. Thousands of visitors and residents of San Luis Obispo County have been exposed to the natural resources of the area through outings led by members of the Santa Lucia Chapter. The Chapter establishes and maintains local trails, participates in local governmental decisions, promotes conservation, publishes a periodic newsletter, and holds monthly meetings which are open to the public.

We firmly believe that the public should be fully informed and involved in all decisions which affect the environment. Membership in the Sierra Club includes a subscription to *Sierra*, the Club's national magazine, as well as the *Santa Lucian*, the Chapter newsletter, which offers information on local outings and activities. For additional information, check our website: www.sierraclub.org/chapters/santalucia.

The Santa Lucia Chapter relies entirely on volunteers for its activities. Local Chapter members have built or improved many trails in the area, including the Felsman Loop, Bishop Peak Trail, Poly "P" Trail, and Eagle Rock Nature Trail. The Chapter was instrumental in creating the Bishop Peak Preserve and the Garcia Wilderness, and in the preservation of the Morros. We have worked with local governments to preserve other areas of the Central Coast, including Hearst Ranch, East-West Ranch, Diablo Canyon, the city of San Luis Obispo's greenbelt, and Guadalupe-Nipomo Dunes.

The Trail Guide is also strictly a volunteer effort. It was first published in 1981 to acquaint the public with the unspoiled beauty of San Luis Obispo County. This revision has sought to update information and to offer a wider choice of outings. Last but not least, we hope you will join us in our mission: "to explore, enjoy, and protect our planet."

SANTA LUCIA
MOUNTAINS

FOSTER

Natural History of San Luis Obispo County

Geology and Geography

Much of the ground we walk on in San Luis Obispo County was once part of an ancient sea floor, dating back to the Jurassic period, some 180 million years ago. The trails of the area give abundant evidence of this. The old sea floor is visible as the deep rocks on the Cerro Alto and Poly Canyon Trails. Some of it was squeezed into a deep trench on the edge of the continent, where it fragmented into large blocks. Some was crushed by unimaginable forces, stirred up to the surface, and churned into a rock called melange, best described as a massive fruitcake. Melange can be seen on trails at El Chorro Regional Park and in the large masses of blue-green serpentine (the California state rock) near Laguna Lake. Mixed with relatively undeformed sandstone, melange is also visible on the Leffingwell Landing Trail near San Simeon.

In the eastern part of the county, we find rocks belonging to the old continent. Granite is especially apparent on the Fernandez Trail. Sand, washed westward around 100 million years ago and loosely compressed, formed sandstone, which covers the granite of the old sea floor. Sandstone is abundant in La Panza Range .

A period of relative peace followed, between 65 and 20 million years ago, when the land was lifted up out of the water and gradually eroded by wind and rain. This period left little trace in the rocks. With the return of the ocean, large volcanoes formed along the SLO-Morro Rock line. Their plugged-up remnants, the Morros (Spanish for "hills"), can be seen from the two Morro Bay State Park trails as well as from Highway 1 and Los Osos Valley Road. Although there are really nine Morros, locals call them the "Seven Sisters."

The Morros   Standing guard at the entrance of Morro Bay, **Morro Rock** is the most visible and most photographed of the Nine Sisters. Besides drawing tourists, it is now an ecological reserve and home to the peregrine falcon. To the southeast, the next peak we find is **Black Hill**, which gets its name from a tar seep on its north side. It lies behind Morro Bay State Park and is covered by chaparral. East of South Bay Boulevard we find **Cerro Cabrillo**, really two peaks of nearly equal height. Its base extends into the

Morro Bay salt marsh. **Hollister Peak**, highest from base to top, is a photogenic rock formation which lies east of Cerro Cabrillo. Golden eagles gracefully circle the summit, where they have been known to nest. Southeast of Cuesta College lies the distinctive summit of **Cerro Romauldo**. The next two Morros are popular with rock climbers: **Chumash Peak**, made of a few very large boulders, and **Bishop Peak**, the tallest of the Nine Sisters at 1559 feet, just north of Foothill Boulevard. **Cerro San Luis** lies close by, to the south of Foothill Boulevard. Finally, **Islay Hill**, a round grassy volcanic cone, rises out of Edna Valley near the airport. More information and photos can be accessed on the Web, www.santalucia.sierraclub.org.

Marine Basins

20 million years ago, faulting caused a series of marine basins to form. The best example in the area is the present Santa Barbara Channel. These basins were created, in part, by the action of the San Andreas Fault. This movement of the earth's crust ultimately transferred parts of the county from the Palm Springs area to their present position. The basins slowly filled with sedimentary rock. Miocene rocks can be seen in Lopez Canyon, Big Falls and Little Falls Trails. The near-white, flinty Monterey Formation along the East Cuesta Ridge also dates back to the Miocene era.

The coastal basins were compressed, and the sediments were faulted and folded at the end of the Pliocene Epoch, forming the foothills and mountains we see today. Such faulted sediments can be seen at Montaña de Oro State Park. At the end of the Pliocene Epoch sediment from the rising mountains formed giant alluvial fans in the Edna Valley and Paso Robles-Shandon area, now mere gravel flats obscured by ongoing crustal movement.

The process of forming and molding the mountains and valleys continues today. The ocean has fallen and risen with the growth and melting of ice sheets, sometimes dropping hundreds of feet and leaving broad coastal plains to the west of our present beaches. Sand blown from the plain, especially as the sea advanced eastward, has formed the Nipomo and Morro Bay sandspit dunes. The latter have also been replenished with sand carried from the north and south ends of Estero Bay by wave-driven currents.

As viewed today, the county is crossed by a series of mountain ranges laid out northwest to southeast, roughly parallel to the coast. The Santa Lucia Range extends the entire length of the county and includes some of its highest peaks. The Salinas River headwaters separate the Santa Lucias from the La Panza Mountains to the east. Beyond La Panza Mountains stretches an arid plateau called Carrisa Plains. The Temblor Range to the east owes its name to the earth movements of the San Andreas Fault, which runs through the Carrisa Plains. A southern extension of the La Panza Range is called the Caliente Range. It stretches between the Cuyama Valley and the Carrisa Plains and includes 5,106-foot Caliente Mountain, the county's highest peak.

Standing on the crest of La Panza Range one's eye can follow the San Andreas Fault as it runs down the Carrisa Plains, and look across to the North American Plate. Most of San Luis Obispo County is on a different continental plate, called the Salinian Block, that is moving northwestward at a rate of four centimeters per year, a slice of North America caught on the Pacific Plate. It moves not gently but in spurts, which we know as earthquakes. The last earthquake of geological significance occurred in 1966 at Parkfield. In a few million years the hills of San Francisco will doubtless slide past on the eastern side of San Luis Obispo County.

Climate

West of the Santa Lucia Mountains, the Pacific Ocean largely determines the weather. Oceanic influence in this area is felt as cool summers and mild winters. Cool summers are largely due to increased cloudiness or summer fog, generated by warm inland air condensing near the coast.

Summers east of the Santa Lucias are hotter and drier than on the coast, with cooler nights. July and August are the driest months, November to April the wettest. The heaviest rains fall in the North Coast area above Cambria, in Santa Margarita, and in the city of San Luis Obispo, where storms are blown up and over Cuesta Grade. Rainfall in San Luis Obispo is typically 16 to 18 inches a year, though as much as 50 inches has been recorded.

East of the mountains, precipitation drops off sharply because clouds are "wrung out" as they pass over higher elevations. Soda Lake is the driest area in the county, averaging 8 to 9 inches annual rainfall. Inland areas, away from the moderating influence of the ocean, regularly experience subfreezing temperatures in winter.

Plants and Wildlife

The varied topography and climates of San Luis Obispo County combine to make possible a great variety of plants and animals, some of which are native to the area. Their scientific names ring with a certain familiarity, for example: *Arctostaphylos morroensis* (Morro manzanita, found on sandy soils south of Morro Bay), *Fremontia obispoensis* (Obispo flannel

15

bush, found on Cuesta Ridge) and *Lupinus nipomoensis* (Nipomo dunes lupine). The official flower of San Luis Obispo County, *Lupinus ludovicianus* (San Luis lupine), is also native to the drier hills of the central coast.

San Luis Obispo County offers a great diversity of living forms. Over 400 species of birds may live in or pass through this county in a typical year. Impressive numbers of plants and animals are found in the local tidepools, and the oak woodlands support thousands of terrestrial species. By hiking the trails listed in this guide you will encounter life forms adapted to a wide range of conditions, from sandy intertidal zones to mountain forests and to arid, alkaline sinks.

Closest to the sea one finds tidepools, rock outcroppings colonized by algae of many shapes, sizes, and colors, and populated by invertebrates such as sea anemones, mussels, barnacles, snails and crabs. Two birds, the black oystercatcher and the black turnstone, make their living from the mussel beds and the small creatures crawling among them. Montaña de Oro State Park and the San Simeon coast provide easy access to the greatest concentration of tidepools in the county.

Coastal birds, such as pelicans and cormorants, fish for food in the open waters. Gulls forage along the shore, and in summer vast flocks of sooty shearwater, an open ocean bird, can be seen feeding on schools of small fish just offshore. Sandpipers probe the shoreline to find small creatures that burrow in the sand. At Morro Rock a breeding pair of endangered peregrine falcons swoop down like bullets to catch smaller birds in mid-air.

Morro Bay Inside the bay, protected from wave action and strong winds, one finds mud flats and a salt marsh. Eel grass grows in the bay itself, on the mud flat, while pickleweed, sea lavender, and salt grass are among the plants found in the salt marsh. The marsh is a haven for numerous coastal birds and is one of the last unspoiled estuaries left along the California coast. Herons and egrets feed in the shallows. Sandpipers are found in great numbers on the mud flats, especially in winter. Ducks, grebes, loons and cormorants live on the bay, as does the controversial and endangered sea otter.

The Dunes Surrounding Morro Bay, and from Pismo Beach south into Santa Barbara County, the coast is dominated by sand dunes. The dunes support sensitive plant communities, low-growing succulents near the ocean and small shrubs further inland. Among these are California sagebrush, sea rocket, mock heather, deerweed, sand verbena and the endangered San Luis Obispo monardella and Nipomo lupine. The coast horned lizard and the rare snowy plover, camouflaged by their sandy color,

16

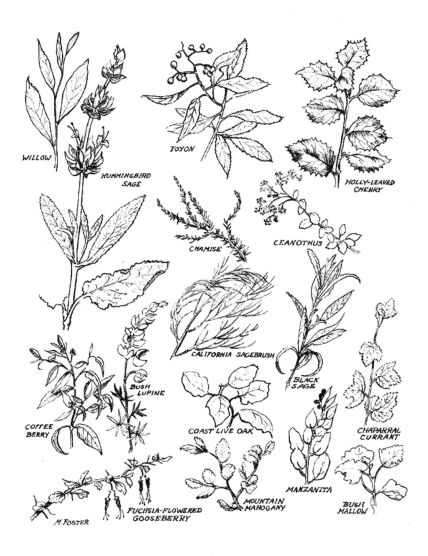

WILLOW
TOYON
HUMMINGBIRD SAGE
HOLLY-LEAVED CHERRY
CHAMISE
CEANOTHUS
CALIFORNIA SAGEBRUSH
BUSH LUPINE
BLACK SAGE
COFFEE BERRY
COAST LIVE OAK
CHAPARRAL CURRANT
MANZANITA
FUCHSIA-FLOWERED GOOSEBERRY
MOUNTAIN MAHOGANY
BUSH MALLOW
M. FOSTER

inhabit the dunes. Near Los Osos, the endangered Morro Bay kangaroo rat inhabits dune plant communities; the endangered least tern nests on beaches near the mouth of the Santa Maria River.

Grassland   Areas disturbed by agriculture, fire or grazing become grasslands, often punctuated by coast live oak, blue or valley oaks, and gray (digger) pine. Most of the grasses are invasive species imported from Europe, although a few areas of native grasses survive. These California savannas offer world-famous wildflower displays from March through April. Grassland fauna include western fence lizards, California ground squirrels, weasels, badgers, pocket gophers, and meadow voles. Bird species that

17

make grassland their habitat include white-throated swifts, swallows, sparrows, red-tailed hawks, golden eagles, American kestrels, larks and loggerhead shrikes.

Scrub and Chaparral If left undisturbed, coastal grasslands will give way to low growing, gray-green shrubs known collectively as coastal sage scrub. Black sage, California sagebrush, coyote bush, artemisia and golden yarrow grow here.

Where the land is steeper and drier the hills are covered by chaparral. Chaparral is taller and thicker than coastal sage scrub, with tough leathery leaves. Dense chaparral growth may form an impenetrable barrier. Dominant chaparral shrubs are chamise, sticky bush monkey flower, ceanothus and manzanita. Inland chaparral, more varied than coastal vegetation, includes silk tassle bush, toyon, buck brush, woolly blue curls and squaw bush.

Many creatures make their home among chaparral and coastal scrub: western fence and whiptail lizards, black-tailed jackrabbit, cottontail, California pocket mouse, woodrat, coastal mule deer, California quail, Anna's hummingbird, wrentit, scrub jay, California thrasher, rufous-sided and brown towhees and white-crowned sparrows.

Forests Coastal scrub is bordered by forests of closed-cone conifers, so named because the cones do not open immediately but stay on the tree until it dies. In San Luis Obispo County these forests are found in three areas: Coon Creek Canyon in Montaña de Oro State Park, where Bishop pines crowd the steep slopes; Cambria, where the southernmost natural extension of Monterey pines is found; and the east and west slopes of Cuesta Grade, home respectively to knob cone pines and Sargent cypress.

Coastal live oak is the most common type of forest in this county, and one of the most diverse of habitats in California. This complex forest consists of roughly four levels: at the top are coastal live oak trees; below their canopy grow tall shrubs, mostly toyon and coffeeberry; below these is a layer of short shrubs—poison oak, currant, gooseberry and sticky bush monkey flower; and finally a ground layer of herbs, grasses, and ferns. In forests where cattle are allowed to graze, grasses and ferns may replace the shrub layers. In some areas native vegetation has been replaced by eucalyptus, an Australian import. Large eucalyptus groves, especially in San Simeon, Los Osos, Oceano and the Nipomo mesa, attract spectacular displays of monarch butterflies in late spring.

On the high mountain slopes of the coast ranges, vegetation changes to mixed evergreen forests and interior closed-cone conifer forests. Mixed evergreen forests occupy the canyons, the moist north and east slopes, and the highest summits. These forests are complex and varied. Black oak, sugar pine and yellow pine are predominantly found in the northern forests. Madrone, coast live oak, big leaf maple and Coulter pine dominate the southern forests.

In the eastern interior basins, rolling grasslands are peppered with valley oak, blue oak, and digger pine. Canopies of live oak follow stream courses. These California savannas offer world-famous spring wildflower shows from late March through April.

Living within these forests and woodlands, on the coast and inland, are the California newt, slender salamander, alligator lizard, cottontail, western gray squirrel, deer mouse, raccoon, coastal mule deer, mountain lion, bobcat, acorn woodpecker, bushtit, northern flicker, mourning dove, great horned owl and California quail. The wild turkey inhabits grassland and dense forest alike. The yellow-billed magpie is a showy resident of deciduous oak forests.

Rivers and Streams A special ecological community exists in the valley of the Salinas and its tributaries, and to a lesser extent in streams nearer the coast. This is the riparian or stream-side woodland. It includes plants adapted to year-round water: willows, sycamores, cottonwoods, California bay, big-leaf maple, coast live oak and the ubiquitous poison oak. Pacific tree frogs flourish in riparian woodland, along with alligator lizards, garter snakes, opossums, raccoons, deer mice, beavers, muskrats, cottontails, black bears, Cooper's hawks, woodpeckers and song sparrows.

We should mention vernal pools, depressions that hold water only for a brief time in the spring. Good examples are found along Pozo Road east of Santa Margarita. Plants that grow here must adapt to beginning life in water and ending it under conditions resembling a baked clay pot. Unusual flowers like meadow foam and downingia survive in this setting.

Soda Lake The extensive alkali sink around Soda Lake resembles a coastal salt marsh in many ways. Its plant species belong to the same families as those in the coastal salt marsh, even though they may have evolved into a different appearance. The rare Lost Hills saltbush grows here. Pintail ducks, Canadian geese, black-necked stilts, American avocets, northern harriers, mountain bluebirds and sage sparrows are common in cooler weather. In winter the area hosts spectacular displays of sandhill cranes, hawks, eagles, falcons and curlews. The panoramic views of wide-open spaces and mountains are breathtaking.

Surrounding the alkali sink is arid grassland punctuated by California buckwheat and salt bush. The east side is home to several endangered animals, including ground squirrel, San Joaquin kit fox, giant kangaroo rat, San Joaquin antelope, and blunt-nosed leopard lizard. Sharing this habitat are spadefoot toads, sideblotched lizards, black-tailed jackrabbits, badgers and long-tailed weasels. Many kinds of hawks, American kestrels, and golden eagles prey on the smaller creatures. The western kingbird, meadowlark and horned lark also inhabit the area.

Juniper/Grassland Mix The eastern mountains and valleys contain plants adapted to little rain and hot summers. Interior dry hills are home to California juniper, a shrub or small tree. Scattered shrubs of California buckwheat, Douglas shrubby groundsel and golden bushes grow here with grasses and herbs in between. Although extremely hot in summer, this area is pleasant for hiking in winter and late spring.

Wildlife: Past and Future

Many changes have taken place in San Luis Obispo County in a relatively short time. No more than 150 years ago large herds of tule elk and pronghorn antelope roamed the grasslands of the eastern county. Names such as Antelope Springs and Elkhorn Plain are reminders of their existence. The elk and pronghorn (fastest animal in North America) supported great numbers of large predators such as coyotes, wolves and grizzly bears. Before 1850, grizzly bears were the dominant predators of coastal California. Written accounts by early Spanish explorers suggest that areas such as Los Osos ("The Bears") and Oso Flaco ("Thin Bear") had greater densities of grizzlies than any other place in California. By 1890, with over-hunting and human settlement, the grizzly was gone from this county.

The California condor was once commonly seen in the eastern plains of the county, but in the 1980s the last of their kind were trapped for a captive breeding program. The vegetation, too, has changed. Before the turn of the century the trip through Chorro Valley by horse and wagon from the city of San Luis Obispo to Morro Bay was an all-day venture through dense coastal scrub communities. Today non-native grasslands predominate. The native grasses of California, which include long-lived bunch grasses, are nearly all gone, the result of competition from introduced species.

What will the future be like for San Luis Obispo County? Surely changes will continue in this developing area. But there are several bright spots to be considered. Concerned citizens and county leaders have worked to acquire lands that are preserved as parks, trailways and wildlife habitats.

This decade marked the reintroduction of the tule elk and pronghorn antelope into Cuyama Valley and Carrisa Plains after a century of absence. With continued effort and farsightedness, San Luis Obispo County will remain a place where wildlife and people can coexist.

Archaeology

Aborigines occupied San Luis Obispo County at least 9,000 years ago. Among them were the tall, bronzed, attractive Chumash and Salinans. The boundary between these groups probably shifted at various times, from Cuesta Ridge to Ragged Point, depending on changing conditions of climate, food and water. Accurate information on these early Indians is limited because less than ten per cent of the county has been surveyed and only about a dozen scientific excavations have been made.

Evidence of prehistoric life along these trails is abundant. The hiker may notice parabolic depressions in boulders and rock outcroppings. These are bedrock mortars probably used by the early Indians to grind acorns. Please leave them undisturbed. Deposits of shells, or middens, may be seen in the sand dunes. Most were created by Indians processing the shellfish for food. Please do not walk, remove shells, or dig in the middens you may find. They are fragile and need your cooperation to be saved for future generations.

Other types of sites—such as hunting blinds, fish traps or dams, chipping and quarry sites, trails and cemeteries—contain clues that can add to knowledge, but only an expert can extract the information and record it accurately. Thus, it is important to leave everything intact in its original site. Call the San Luis Obispo County Archaeological Society (543-7831) to report discoveries.

SLOCAS sponsors free public lectures on archaeology at various locations in the area. Meetings are announced in local media. Call above number for information, or write SLOCAS, P.O. Box 109, San Luis Obispo, California 93406. The Indian museum at Cuesta can be visited by appointment.

Upper Lopez Canyon Trail

Hiking in
San Luis Obispo County

State Parks and National Forests

The many trails of San Luis Obispo County are found in city parks and reserves, county parks, California State parks and beaches, Los Padres National Forest, privately held lands, and in property held by various land trusts and conservation organizations.

The trails described in this guide cover only those trails open to the general public. A few heavily-used trails are not described here out of respect for the property owners. These include the beautiful route to the top of San Luis Mountain (erroneously called Madonna Mountain) and challenging High School Hill. The Sierra Club strongly discourages hiking on private property at any time unless prior permission is obtained from the ranch manager or landowner.

The California Department of Parks and Recreation maintains 12,530 acres in San Luis Obispo County, divided among a dozen properties: eight beaches, two parks, Los Osos Oaks State Reserve and Hearst San Simeon State Historical Monument. This guide includes all state park areas in the county that offer good hiking opportunities. To protect wildlife, dogs are prohibited on park trails. Collection or removal of plants is also prohibited.

Montaña de Oro State Park

The largest of these state properties is the 8,000-acre Montaña de Oro State Park, a relatively unspoiled stretch of rocky shoreline and sheltered coves. Its rugged 60-foot cliffs are topped by a series of alluvial terraces that slope up to the peaks of the San Luis Range.

The park name, "mountain of gold" in Spanish, comes from the park's dazzling carpets of yellow wildflowers. Fiddlenecks, goldfields and California poppies grow on the plains; sticky bush monkey flowers, tidy tips and California buttercups inhabit the slopes.

To get to the park from Highway 101, drive 12 miles northwest on Los Osos Valley Road. From Highway 1, take the Los Osos-Baywood Park exit, turn south onto South Bay Boulevard, and drive to its termination at Los Osos Valley Road and turn right. The road turns south to become Pecho

Road and leads into the park. The park headquarters is 2.7 miles inside the park entrance on a bluff overlooking Spooner's Cove. This frame building was the Spooner family home starting in 1892 when the area was used for farming and ranching.

Morro Bay State Park

Morro Bay State Park, south of the city of Morro Bay, consists of 1,905 acres adjoining the bay for which it is named. The park includes a portion of the Morro Bay estuary, one of the largest natural salt marshes on the California coast, which attracts more than 250 species of birds. The park is dotted with pine, eucalyptus and other trees, many of them planted in the 1930s by the California Conservation Corps.

To reach the park, drive 12 miles north of San Luis Obispo on Highway 1. Take the Los Osos-Baywood Park exit, turn south on South Bay Boulevard, and go south .9 mile to the park entrance on the right. The park may also be entered from the south end of Main Street in Morro Bay.

The Morro Bay Museum of Natural History is inside the Morro Bay State Park at White Point. Operated by the California Parks and Recreation Department with the aid of volunteer docents, it features natural history displays and films. Books and pamphlets on natural history, including local publications, are sold in the museum foyer. The museum is open every day except Thanksgiving, Christmas and New Year's Day from 10 a.m. to 5 p.m. The California Department of Parks and Recreation sponsors nature walks led by docents and rangers at the Morro Bay and Montaña de Oro State Parks and at Pismo State Beach. More information on the state parks and beaches may be obtained on the Internet at http://cal-parks.ca.gov/, or by contacting:

California Parks and Recreation Dept.
San Luis Obispo Coast District Office
3220 South Higuera St., Suite 311
San Luis Obispo, California 93401
(805) 549-3312
Hours: Monday to Friday, 8 a.m. to 5 p.m.
Montaña de Oro State Park, (805) 528-0513
Morro Bay State Park, (805) 772-2560
Museum of Natural History, (805) 772-2694
(www.mbspmuseum.org)
Pismo State Beach (805) 489-2684

Los Padres National Forest

Those portions of the Los Padres National Forest within San Luis Obispo County include 190,000 acres of mountainous terrain. Starting north of Highway 41 between Atascadero and Morro Bay, the forest extends along the crest of the Santa Lucia Range to the Cuyama River and south into Santa Barbara County. An arm of the forest encompasses La Panza Range east of Santa Margarita.

Along Lopez Canyon, in the heart of the forest east of San Luis Obispo, lies the 21,678-acre Santa Lucia Wilderness. It was created through the efforts of the Sierra Club under the 1978 Endangered American Wilderness Act. Human intrusion in this zone is limited in order to preserve its natural state, solitude and resources.

Pine-crowned peaks, majestic rocky crags and views of the snow-capped Sierras characterize the Machesna Wilderness. The 20,000 acre wilderness became part of our National Wilderness System in 1984. Chaparral oak woodlands and conifer forests blanket its rugged terrain. The Wilderness contains a 1,500 acre Research Natural Area dedicated to the study of a unique strain of Coulter pine. Besides Coulter pine, this area is well-forested with interior live oak, blue oak, scrub oak, and many representatives of the chaparral community. It is also one of the most interesting wildflower areas in California. Prairie falcon, deer, mountain lion, black bear and tule elk make their home in the undisturbed landscape. Part of the wilderness is designated critical habitat for the California condor. A unique wilderness experience awaits the hiker 25 miles from San Luis Obispo.

Natural scenic beauty abounds in the Garcia Wilderness, established in 1992, a 14,100-acre wilderness located between the Santa Lucia and Machesna Wilderness areas. Besides solitude and outstanding panoramic views, the area includes a variety of plant communities: meadows, grasslands, rugged chaparral-covered slopes and lush creekside vegetation. In spring, an extravagant display of wildflowers coats the hillsides.

Information on road and trail conditions may be obtained from the District Ranger's Office, 1616 Carlotti Drive, Santa Maria, CA 93454, phone (805) 925-9538. Wilderness permits are required to enter the wilderness areas in the Los Padres National Forest. Obtain permits at the San Luis Obispo Chamber of Commerce, Los Padres Ranger Station in Santa Maria, or log onto www.R5.PSWFS.GOV/lospadres.

Trail Conditions

The condition of trails throughout San Luis Obispo County, as elsewhere, can vary greatly with time and changing seasons. The volunteers who created this book have hiked each and every trail described here. However, we advise the hiker, biker, or horseback rider to check on trail conditions prior to setting out on a wilderness trek. Please use common sense and good judgment, and pay attention to warnings in this book and elsewhere. Poor judgment and unnecessary risk taking endanger not only your life but that of rescue crews. Above all, the Sierra Club aims to make everyone's wilderness experience safe and enjoyable.

Hazards

Hiking in San Luis Obispo County, as elsewhere, includes a few hazards along with many rewards. Poison oak, rattlesnakes and wood ticks are commonly encountered, as well as mountain lions. Some animals carry rabies or plague, so avoid contact with all animals, dead or alive. Also, refrain from tasting or touching any unknown plant. Small children especially should be watched at all times.

Poison Oak

Poison oak flourishes through-out the Central Coast, especially in moist areas, eroded ravines and shady chaparral slopes. Its form varies: it may be a climbing vine or a squat shrub. Its leaves are one to four inches long, usually lobed and alternate along the smooth stem in clusters of three. Small yellow-green, star-shaped flowers appear in clusters at the ends of new growth in spring when the leaves are a vivid, glistening green. In late summer and early fall the leaves change to crimson. After they drop, there may be tight clusters of small waxy berries on the stem.

Poison Oak

Most parts of the plant contain a yellowish oil that produces an itchy rash and possibly blisters. This oil is potent until removed, whether the carrier is skin, clothing, a dead plant or pet fur. Sensitivity to the toxin varies from person to person, but usually increases with age and repeated exposure to poison oak. Do not become overly confident of immunity to poison oak. It has been known to disappear suddenly and without warning.

Don't brush against any part of the plant or allow a pet to touch it. Though the danger is greatest in spring and summer, the less noticeable, bare stems in winter can also transmit the toxic oil. This potent oil also may be carried by the smoke of burning poison oak branches.

Treatment: As soon as possible after exposure, clean skin with rubbing alcohol, and then wash thoroughly in cool water with an alkaline yellow laundry soap. Do not use a cosmetic or oily soap. Rinse thoroughly, and pat dry gently. Wash all contaminated clothing, including sides and soles of shoes. Heavy exposure requires medical attention.

Rattlesnakes

The Southern Pacific Western rattlesnake is abundant throughout San Luis Obispo County. It is found most often in shaded areas during hot days and in warm areas during cool weather. It has a heavy body and a long triangular head on a slender neck. Adult rattlers are 20 to 55 inches long. Not all rattlesnakes have rattles, so don't count on them for identification.

The bite mark of a rattle-snake shows one or two large fang punctures and possibly some smaller tooth marks. These punctures may or may not bleed. The immediate reaction is usually a burning pain, then increased pain, swelling and discoloration. Children are especially likely to have severe reactions because of their small body weight.

Western Diamond Rattlesnake

Rattlesnakes try to avoid contact with people but will fight if cornered or surprised. Wear heavy socks and high boots with trouser legs outside the boots. Watch hands and feet, especially when rock climbing; rattlers often sun themselves on a rock. Poke a stick in a crevice before exploring it with fingers, and look before stepping over a big log. If a rattler is heard, stand still until its whereabouts is known. Walk slowly away—don't jump or run blindly.

Treatment: The most important step is to keep the victim calm. Wash the wound if possible. It is essential to slow the flow of venom by avoiding panic and keeping the bitten area immobilized, below heart level. The victim should walk slowly or preferably be carried out.

Get medical help as soon as possible. If the victim cannot receive medical help within 30 minutes, consider suctioning the wound using a snakebite kit. Do not apply ice, cut the wound, or use a tourniquet. If the snake can be killed without risk or delay, it should be brought to the hospital for identification.

Wood and Deer Ticks

Wood and deer ticks are usually found on warm, brush-covered southerly slopes. They hang from shrubs until they detect carbon dioxide from passing animals or people. They are present all year long, but become more prevalent after first fall rains. Large enough to be seen with the naked eye, ticks usually crawl around on the skin before biting, so check body and clothing during the wet season. Bites may produce itching, painful sores and are carriers of Lyme Disease. Wood ticks carry Rocky Mountain spotted fever, which can be fatal if untreated.

Deer ticks carry Lyme Disease, rare in California, but expected to become more prevalent with time Recent studies have shown it takes 24-48 hours of continuous contact after a tick has bitten before it transfers disease to humans. Symptoms calling for medical attention are a rash, flu-like symptoms, or a bulls'-eye appearance around the bite. If such symptoms appear, see a physician for treatment. In any case, see a physician if you are unsure how long a tick has been attached.

Don't handle rodents. Avoid sitting or lying among dried leaves where tick-infested animals may have bedded down. Avoid old hollow logs, rotting stumps and other small rodent homes. If you find a dead animal on the trail, especially a rodent, stay away from it and notify a ranger.

Treatment: If a tick is seen crawling on clothing or skin, pick it off. Don't crush it with fingers because of the danger of infection. If it has become embedded, scrape off with a credit card or grasp it near the head as close to the skin as possible with a pair of tweezers, and pull with gentle, steady pressure. The tick may eventually weaken and let go. This may take several minutes. If the tick has been removed, clean the wound with an antiseptic such as alcohol and dress with antibiotics, and watch for signs of infection. In some cases, the tick is too deeply embedded. It may then be necessary to seek medical help.

Beware of popular methods for removing ticks—turning the tick counter-clockwise to "unscrew" it, applying heat or a match to the rear end of the tick to make it back out, and so on. These methods cause more harm than good. The tick's head can break off under the skin and remain as a source of infection, and heat may force the tick to release infectious material below the skin.

Rabies and Plague

Rabies is a deadly viral disease most commonly associated with skunks and bats but also carried by other mammals. Transmission is usually via bites, but rabies can also be contracted by allowing broken skin to come into contact with saliva or other body fluids from infected animals.

Plague is a bacterial disease transmitted by fleas carried by rodents, such as squirrels and rabbits. Though it can now be treated by antibiotics, it is still a serious disease and can be fatal.

Sick animals are particularly likely to come close to people while their healthy relatives keep their distance. Any nocturnal animal seen out during the daytime is a rabies suspect. Avoid contact with any wild mammals or carcasses of mammals, and keep dogs from doing so.

Treatment: If bitten by any animal, seek medical attention. Also seek medical attention if it is believed exposure to plague has occurred or if symptoms develop, such as high fever, chills or prostration.

Topographic Maps

The location maps included in this guide are provided for general orientation only and are not intended to replace topographic (topo) maps. A topo map is recommended for even a modest outing, and essential for back-country and cross-country outings. In an emergency it can be a lifesaver.

The U.S. Geological Survey (USGS) publishes topographic maps that depict with considerable accuracy roads, lakes, rivers, and streams, trails, forests, principal structures and elevations. A system of standard symbols and colors identifies landmarks and vegetation. Contour lines indicate elevations. These maps are plotted to scale. Used along with a compass and guidebook, they add safety and interest to any outing.

Topo maps for trails described in this guide may be purchased at sporting goods stores such as Mountain Air and Granite Stairway, printed or on CD-ROM. A wide selection of USGS maps in on reserve in the document section of the Robert E. Kennedy Library, Cal Poly State University. The maps may be ordered on the Web at http://mcmcweb.er.usgs.gov/topomaps/ordering_maps.html, or by contacting:

U.S. Geological Survey-Branch of Distribution Federal Center
Box 25286
Denver, Colorado 80225
(888) 275-8747
(303)202-4700
fax (303) 202-4693

U.S. Geological Survey will, on request, send a free index map of California. The map shows an outline of the state divided into named rectangles, each of which is portrayed on a separate topo map. Pamphlet "GPO-SN-024-001-02793-3", describing topo maps and symbols also, is available free on request.

The USGS publishes several series of maps. All maps mentioned in this guide are in the 7.5 minute series, the most widely used, where 2.5 inches equals one mile. For convenience in handling, it is suggested that you make a photocopy of the part of the map covering your hike and mark its magnetic north. This makes it easier to carry and it can be marked en route, while preserving the original.

A map of the Los Padres National Forest is sold at all local Forest Service offices.

Please note: **Trail conditions change with time and seasons. For your own safety, use topo maps and check with rangers in advance.**

Every effort has been made to give accurate information and guidance. However, the location maps are no substitute for topographic maps or for current information from park rangers and experienced hikers. It is not advisable to hike alone due to the danger of accidents, sudden illness, or assaults. The Santa Lucia Chapter of the Sierra Club assumes no responsibility for your safety when hiking. Please be careful.

Trail Classification

Easy

Black Hill
East-West Ranch
Guiton (Oceano Lagoon)
Jim Green
Los Osos Oaks Reserve
Moonstone Beach
Ragged Point
Reservoir Flats
Stenner Creek
Sweet Springs Nature Preserve

Eagle Rock
Elfin Forest
Islay Hill Open Space
Laguna Lake Park
Montaña de Oro Bluff
Oso Flaco Lake
Reservoir Canyon
San Simeon
South Hills Open Space
Terrace Hill

Easy to Moderate

Coon Creek
Maino Open Space

Felsman Loop

Moderate

Bishop Peak
Blinn Ranch
Cerro Alto Long Hike
East Cuesta Ridge
Grey Pine-Vaca Flat Loop
Hi Mountain
Poly "P" Loop
Poly Canyon Loop
Ridge-Barranca Loop
Rocky Point
Trout Creek to Buckeye Camp
Valencia Peak

Black Hill Loop
Cabrillo Peaks
Cerro Alto Short Hike
Fernandez
Islay Creek
Morro Bay Sandspit

Prefumo Canyon
Rinconada Mine
Sandstone
Tuouski-Two Waters

Moderately Strenuous

Adobe
Caldwell to Buckeye
Gifford Ranch
Little Falls
Oats Peak-Coon Creek Loop

Big Falls
False Alan Peak
Hi Valley
Lopez Canyon
Stony Creek

Strenuous

American Canyon
Machesna

Caliente Mountain

Rules of the Trail

Hikers yield to horses.

Mountain bikers yield to horses and hikers.

In order not to spook horses,
stand still on the downhill side of the trail as they pass.

Keep dogs on leash to protect wildlife, livestock and hikers.

Pick up your trash. Take only pictures, leave only footprints.

TRAILS

CERRO ALTO TRAIL

Cambria
San Simeon

East-West Ranch
Moonstone Beach
Ragged Point
San Simeon Trail

MOONSTONE BEACH
CAMBRIA

M·R·FOSTER

East-West Ranch

East-West Ranch

Usage:	Hikers Only
Fee:	None
Distance:	1 Mile (One Way)
Approx. Hiking Time:	1 – 2 Hours
Hike Rating:	Easy
USGS Maps:	Cambria

East-West Ranch is a 418-acre reserve acquired by the American Land Conservancy (ALC), and gifted to the Cambria Community Service District (CDS) in the year 2000. Currently, several miles of hiking and biking trails are being planned. At the time of this writing, only one formal trail, the Bluff Trail, is available for public use. Though short, this one-mile walk takes the hiker along spectacular coastline.

Directions to Trailhead: Take Highway 1 north towards Cambria. Turn left (west) on Windsor Boulevard. Follow Windsor past Shamel Park to the end of the road. A parking lot is in the planning stage. At this time, park along the street. The trail is located at the end of Windsor Boulevard.

Moonstone Beach

Usage:	Hikers Only
Fee:	None
Distance:	1 Mile (One Way)
Approx. Hiking Time:	1 – 2 Hours
Hike Rating:	Easy
USGS Maps:	Cambria

The Moonstone Beach Trail explores the bluffs just north of the town of Cambria. It stays about 20 feet above the ocean. This wind-swept bluff offers great views of Piedras Blancas Lighthouse and the ocean north to San Simeon Point before it ends at Leffingwell Landing. On the way one can descend to the beach to explore the many tidepools. At Leffingwell Landing, there used to be an old pier, now torn down. This pier was used from 1874 to 1894 to bring lumber and supplies to residents along San Simeon Creek.

Directions to Trailhead: Take Highway 1 north to Cambria and turn left (west) on Windsor Boulevard. Make an immediate right on Moonstone Beach Drive. Drive 0.3 mile to the Santa Rosa Creek parking lot. The trail is immediately north of the parking lot. There is also a pleasant picnic site at the other end of Moonstone Drive, by the overlook parking area. It has several benches sheltered from the wind.

Ragged Point

Usage:	Hikers Only
Fee:	None
Distance:	1 Mile
Approx. Hiking Time:	0.5 Hours
Hike Rating (Nature Trail):	Easy
USGS Maps:	Burro Mountain

Ragged Point, the southern gateway to the Big Sur coastline, is the northernmost trail in San Luis Obispo County. It offers spectacular views 300 feet above the Pacific Ocean. There are two short trails here; one descends 300 feet to a rocky beach, the other is a 1-mile Nature Trail that contours the edge of the point with excellent views to the north and south. The Ragged Point Inn makes a good lunch stop.

Directions to Trailhead. Take Highway 1 north past Cambria, San Simeon and Piedras Blancas. When Highway 1 begins to make its hairpin turns, Ragged Point is just ahead.

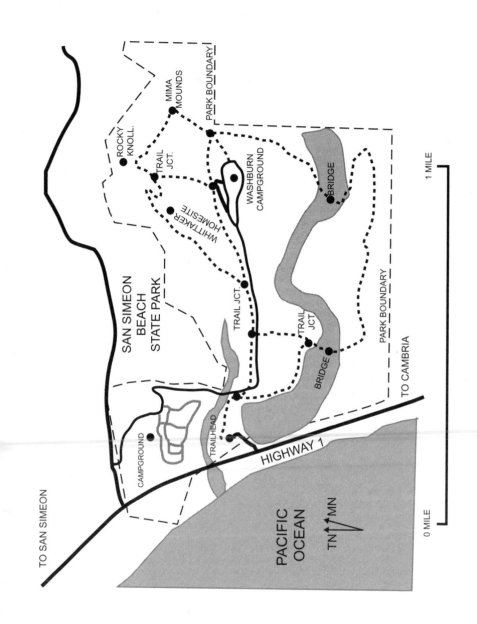

San Simeon

San Simeon

Usage:	Hikers Only
Fee:	None at this Time
Distance:	3.5 Miles (Round Trip)
Elevation Gain/Loss:	500 Feet
Approx. Hiking Time:	2 – 3 Hours
Hike Rating:	Easy
USGS Maps:	San Simeon

Best Time to Hike: All Year

Point On Route:	Distance from Starting Point Miles(Km)	Elevation
San Simeon Trailhead	0.0 (0.0)	100
Bridge across marsh	0.5 (0.8)	100
Enter Forest	0.7 (1.1)	220
Turn down into ravine	1.2 (1.9)	280
Bridge across creek	1.4 (2.2)	160
Campground Junction	1.9 (3.0)	340
Junction w/trail to campground	2.3 (3.7)	300
Whittaker Ranch site	2.5 (4.0)	180
Junction w/trail to campground	2.9 (4.6)	260
Junction w/paved road	3.0 (4.8)	220
Join Main Trail	3.2 (5.1)	100
San Simeon Trailhead	3.5 (5.6)	100

Directions to Trailhead: Take Highway 1 north past Cambria. Turn into the Washburn Day Use Area of the San Simeon State Park Campground. Park in the lot near the public restrooms. The trailhead is 200 yards east of the parking area along a boardwalk, which also leads down to the beach.

Trail Overview: San Simeon State Park was a gift of the Whittaker family many years ago. They came to this area in 1862. This 320-acre ranch was used mainly as a dairy and creamery.

This semi-loop trail explores the old ranch, passing through seasonal marshes, pine forests, riparian habitats and open grasslands. Look for interpretive signs pointing to vernal pools and mima mounds above the upper campground, especially in late winter and early spring. Wildflowers are abundant in season. Deer and raptors frequent the park and may be present any time of day. The park itself is surrounded by the Pacific Ocean to the west and the Coastal Range to the east. Rocky Butte can be seen in the distance high on the ridge. Poison oak may be present along the trail.

The trail is easy to follow and not very strenuous. It makes a great family hike.

Trail Description:

San Simeon Trailhead. Our journey begins a short distance beyond the day use area on a newly constructed boardwalk. Following the east side of a seasonal marsh gives the opportunity to see many bird species, as well as occasional flowers. Reaching the

bridge across the marsh, we can turn either left or right. The left trail will bring us out after our hike through the park. Taking the right fork, we travel across the 300-foot wooden bridge to a short set of stairs as we gradually climb the ridge ahead. The trail now travels through an open meadow with several trail signs. The State Park is working to restore many areas of the park, so please stay on the marked trail. Five hundred feet past the bridge we enter a

forest of Monterey pines. Raptors nest high in the trees above. You may be able to hear the cry of a hawk as it flies overhead. After meandering for 0.5 mile, the trail makes a left turn as it starts its descent into a

ravine on a north-facing slope. Beware of poison oak in this stretch. Also on this slope you will find many ferns, thimble berry, stinging nettle and strawberry plants. The white spots you may see on the low foliage are bird droppings from nests high in the trees. At the bottom of the slope we come to an expansive

bridge more than 500 feet long. It crosses the seasonal marsh, but it is completely surrounded by willows, horsetail ferns and many other trees. The marsh is a prime habitat for many bird species. Once we have crossed the bridge, we come upon what appears to be an old trail up the hill. The main trail continues to the right, following the marsh, as we gradually climb to the ridge of the newly constructed campground. Deer may be spotted in this area. In the distance you can now see the coastal range, including Rocky Butte, the wettest spot in San Luis Obispo County. Reaching the ridge we come to a

trail junction on the east side of the campground. The left fork offers a shortcut that skirts the campground and then rejoins the main trail. Our trail turns right and goes through an opening in the fence, crossing what appears to be an old road. It then reaches a bench and interpretive station. At this station we learn about mima mounds and vernal pools. A prime example of a vernal pool is directly in front of the bench. The trail turns left (west) and starts a slow descent before reaching a large rock on the right, which has probably been used by Chumash and Salinan Indians through the ages. The trail again turns left past a bench and comes to a

junction. The left fork takes us to the campground. Our trail takes the right fork and descends three switchbacks before reaching an old roadway. On this road we again turn left and travel a short distance to the old

Whittaker Ranch site and creamery. This homesite, like many in the area, is surrounded by a grove of eucalyptus trees planted as windbreaks. The dairy products produced here were shipped to San Francisco from the Hearst wharf located in Old San Simeon. Our trail continues with a slow ascent to the ridge. Along this route another interpretive station tells about the Indian peoples that lived in this area. You may also see turkey vultures soaring as if they were playing in the wind. We now come to a

trail junction. The route to the left leads to the campground. This is the route we would have used if we took the shortcut described earlier. Turning right we follow the campground road for 0.2 mile and watch for a

trail sign across the road. You know you are getting close when the bridge we crossed earlier comes into view. At this point turn left, cross the road and walk 0.2 mile down to the bridge and rejoin the

main trail. Turn right and walk 0.4 mile back to the

San Simeon Trailhead, our starting point.

Atascadero

CERRO ALTO TRAIL

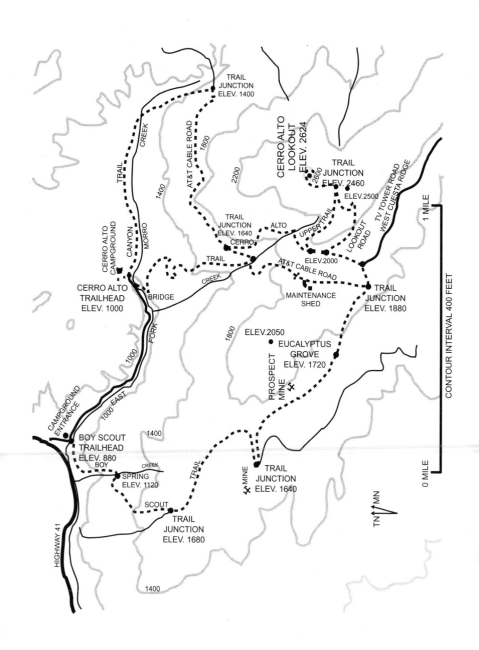

Cerro Alto

Cerro Alto – Long Hike

Usage:	Hikers, Horses, Mountain Bikes and Dogs	
Fee:	Cerro Alto Campground Day Use Fee	
Distance:	7.1 Miles Round Trip	
Elevation Gain/Loss:	+1700/-1700 Feet	
Approx. Hiking Time:	4 Hours	
Hike Rating:	Moderate	
USGS Maps:	Atascadero	

Best Time to Hike: Winter, Spring, Fall, Evenings in Summer

Point On Route:	Distance from Starting Point Miles(Km)	Elevation
Cerro Alto Trailhead	0.0 (0.0)	1020
Morro Creek Crossing	0.5 (0.8)	1240
AT&T Cable Road	1.0 (1.6)	1420
Junction Cerro Alto Summit Trail	1.7 (2.7)	1620
Summit Bypass	2.2 (3.5)	2040
Junction Cerro Alto Summit/ West Cuesta Ridge Trail	2.5 (4.0)	2440
Summit of Cerro Alto	2.8 (4.5)	2620
Junction Cerro Alto Summit/ West Cuesta Ridge Trail	3.1 (5.0)	2440
Summit Bypass	3.4 (5.5)	2020
West Cuesta Ridge Road	3.5 (5.6)	2000
AT&T Cable Road	3.6 (5.8)	1940
Eucalyptus Grove	3.9 (6.3)	1560
Sweetwater Mine Road Junction	4.5 (7.2)	1640
Boy Scout Trail Junction	5.2 (8.4)	1680
Spring	5.7 (9.2)	1200
Cerro Alto Campground Road	6.1 (9.8)	880
Cerro Alto Campground	7.1 (11.4)	1020

Directions to Trailhead: Cerro Alto Campground is located on the south side of Highway 41, 8 miles east of Morro Bay and 12 miles west of Atascadero. Turn into the campground and drive one mile to the Day Use parking area at the back of the campground. There may be a fee for parking in the area. There are two trailheads leaving the Day Use area. Our description starts with the trail on the left immediately across the turnabout at the end of the campground. The other trailhead is immediately behind the restrooms and leads to a wooden bridge.

Trail Overview: This loop trail starts at the campground and climbs through a shaded forest for the first mile, then opens up to chaparral-covered canyons with occasional lush vegetation before reaching the summit of Cerro Alto at elevation 2620'. From the top of Cerro Alto you will get endless views of Morro Bay, Chorro Valley (where the volcanic chain of Nine Sisters or Morros can be seen from Morro Bay to San Luis Obispo), Los Osos, Montaña de Oro and, on a clear day, Mussel Rock in the Guadalupe/Nipomo Dunes. To the northwest, the Cayucos Bluffs and Estero Bay can also be seen. Newts and banana slugs live along the stream, along with many wildflowers during winter and spring, including currant, milk maids, Indian warriors, star lilies, monkey flowers, hound's tongue, virgin bower, bush poppies, ceanothus, and wooly blue curls.

Trail Description:

    Cerro Alto Trailhead. Our route begins at the back of the campground and heads east into a shaded forest of bay trees and oaks. The east fork of Morro Creek is immediately below to our right. The trail comes close to the stream, which offers us a chance to look for creatures swimming in the creek. Leaving the stream, the trail climbs slowly then drops again to

    Morro Creek. The trail crosses the east fork of Morro Creek at this point, which can be a wet ford during the winter months. From here our trail starts a steep climb to the AT&T Cable Road. Maidenhair and other ferns can be found along the route. The area was burned heavily in the Highway 41 fire. You may still have the opportunity to see fire poppies and many star lilies. When you reach the

    AT&T Cable Road, turn right and continue the ascent of Cerro Alto. Within 200 feet, a switchback has been constructed to make this short, steep section of trail a bit easier to climb. We continue to ascend two more small rises before the road levels out. From this point we can view Cerro Alto Campground 600 feet below. Across the valley, an inactive fault runs along the hillside. At the 2.0-mile point we reach the

    Summit Trail Junction. If you wish to take a shorter hike, continue straight for 100 yards and turn right onto a trail that leads back to Cerro Alto Campground. This is called the Margie Cooper Loop.

    Our route turns left here where we will climb another 1000 feet to the

48

summit of Cerro Alto. The climb begins with thick chaparral on both sides. Bush poppies may be blooming along with virgin bower and chaparral pea. Shrubs include scrub oaks, honeysuckle, sage, mint, yucca and yarrow. The trail swings left, then right, crossing a small stream. Continuing our climb, we come to one of the last two shaded spots along our route to the top. Hound's tongue may be found further on the trail. We then round the mountain and reach the

Summit Bypass Trail. This trail connects to the TV Tower Road on West Cuesta Ridge. Our trail turns hard left and continues another 0.4 mile to

Cerro Alto Summit Trail/West Cuesta Trail. We turn left here and climb 0.3 mile to the summit of Cerro Alto at 2624' for a much-needed rest. On top we enjoy sweeping views of San Luis Obispo County. A south view includes Morro Bay, Los Osos, Montaña de Oro, Pismo Dunes, Point Sal, and the Nine Sisters—a chain of volcanic plugs running through the Chorro Valley from Morro Bay to San Luis Obispo. A tenth Morro, Davidson Seamount, 3600 feet high, is found in the Pacific Ocean. Its base is 7600' below sea level. It is the highest of all the Morros and is the first seamount ever to earn its own name. Leaving the summit we retrace our steps to the

Cerro Alto Summit/West Cuesta Trail Junction. This time we take the left fork and descend to TV Tower Road, passing the Summit Bypass Trail on the right. At

West Cuesta Ridge Road, we turn right and walk 200 yards to the

AT&T Road. From here we now head straight instead of turning right. To the left are views of Chorro Valley and San Bernardo Creek drainage. After a short descent we enter a large

Eucalyptus Grove. Once past the first row of trees a large meadow comes into view. This makes a pleasant spot for lunch on a hot day. Our route continues straight, leaving the meadow to our right. The road to the right dead ends. The trail comes to a "Y" junction, where our trail goes left. From here, the trail may get a little faint due to dense growth. But have faith— in less than 50 yards, the trail reaches a motor vehicle stop. Continue past the motor vehicle stop as the trail now enters a chaparral region covered with poppies in spring. You soon reach the

Sweetwater Mine Road Junction. The left fork switchback goes to Sweetwater Mine. Our trail takes the right fork switchback. At the mine junction there are great views of Morro Bay and Los Osos. Following the West Cuesta Ridge Road, the trail is fairly level. We will see Cerro Alto to the east and occasional views of Morro Rock. Watch for a trail fork veering right 0.7 mile from the junction. There may be a trail duck or sign here. This is the

Boy Scout Trail Junction. Take the right fork and begin your descent to Cerro Alto Campground Road. The trail gets rocky and fairly steep here. It will soon turn right and descend deeper into a small ravine reaching an

old spring. The trail crosses the spring, then turns to the left again, descending steeply to the valley below. Now we turn to the right (east) and follow a level trail to the east fork of Morro Creek. You may get your feet wet here trying to cross the creek.

Cerro Alto Campground Road is 50 feet beyond the stream. If you didn't shuttle this trip, turn right and follow Campground Road one mile along the east fork of Morro Creek, back to the Day Use parking area. Please be careful when walking on this twisty road. Motorists cannot see pedestrians far ahead.

On Cerro Alto Trail

Cerro Alto – Short Hike

Usage:	Hikers, Horses, Mountain Bikes and Dogs
Fee:	Cerro Alto Campground Day Use Fee
Distance:	5.1 Miles Round Trip
Elevation Gain/Loss:	+1600/-1600 Feet
Approx. Hiking Time:	4 Hours
Hike Rating:	Moderate
USGS Maps:	Atascadero

Best Time to Hike: Winter, Spring, Fall, Evenings in Summer

Point On Route:	Distance from Starting Point Miles(Km)	Elevation
Cerro Alto Trailhead	0.0 (0.0)	1020
Morro Creek Crossing	0.5 (0.8)	1240
AT&T Cable Road	1.0 (1.6)	1420
Junction Cerro Alto Summit Trail	1.7 (2.7)	1620
Summit Bypass	2.2 (3.5)	2040
Junction Cerro Alto Summit/ West Cuesta Ridge Trail	2.5 (4.0)	2440
Summit of Cerro Alto	2.8 (4.5)	2620
Junction Cerro Alto Summit/ West Cuesta Ridge Trail	3.1 (5.0)	2440
Summit Bypass	3.4 (5.5)	2020
West Cuesta Ridge Road	3.5 (5.6)	2000
AT&T Cable Road	3.6 (5.8)	1940
Cerro Alto Campground Trail Junction	4.3 (6.9)	1560
Cerro Alto Campground	5.1 (8.2)	1020

Directions to Trailhead: Cerro Alto Campground is located on the south side of Highway 41, 8 miles east of Morro Bay and 12 miles west of Atascadero. Turn into the campground and drive one mile to the Day Use parking area at the back of the campground. There may be a fee for parking in the area. There are two trailheads leaving the Day Use area. Our description starts with the trail on the left across the turnabout at the end of the campground. The other trailhead is behind the restrooms and leads to a wooden bridge.

Trail Overview: This loop trail starts at the campground and climbs through a shaded forest for the first mile, then opens up to chaparral-covered canyons with occasional lush vegetation before reaching the summit of Cerro Alto at elevation 2620'. From the top of Cerro Alto the hiker will get endless views of Morro Bay, Chorro Valley (where the volcanic chain of Nine Sisters or Morros can be seen from Morro Bay to San Luis Obispo), Los Osos, Montaña de Oro and, on a clear day, Mussel Rock in the Guadalupe/Nipomo Dunes. To the northwest, the Cayucos Bluffs and Estero Bay can also be seen. Newts and banana slugs may be found along the stream, along with many wildflowers during winter and spring, including currant, milk maids, Indian warriors, star lilies, monkey flowers, hound's tongue, virgin bower, bush poppies, ceanothus and wooly blue curls.

Trail Description:

Cerro Alto Trailhead. Our route begins at the back of the campground and heads east into a shaded forest of bay trees and oaks. The east fork of Morro Creek is immediately below to our right. Look for newts when the trail comes close to the stream. The trail then climbs slowly, then drops again to

Morro Creek. The trail crosses the east fork of Morro Creek at this point, which might be a wet ford during the winter months. From here our trail starts a steep climb to the AT&T Cable Road. Maidenhair and other ferns can be found along the route. This area was burned heavily in the Highway 41 fire. You may still have the opportunity to see fire poppies and many star lilies. When you reach the

AT&T Cable Road, turn right and continue the ascent of Cerro Alto. Within 200 feet, a switchback has been constructed to make this short section of trail a bit easier to climb. We continue to ascend two more small rises before the road levels out. From this point we can view Cerro Alto Campground 600 feet below; also, looking across the valley, one may see evidence of an inactive fault running along the hillside. At the 2.0-mile point we reach the

Summit Trail junction. If you wish to take a shorter hike, continue straight for 100 yards and turn right on to a trail that leads back to Cerro Alto Campground. This is called the Margie Cooper Loop.

Our route turns left here where we will climb another 1000 feet to the summit of Cerro Alto. The trail starts the climb through thick chaparral on both sides. Bush poppies may be in bloom, along with virgin bower and chaparral pea. Shrubs include scrub oaks, honeysuckle, sage, mint, yucca and yarrow. The trail swings left, then right, crossing a small stream. Climbing still, we come to one of the last two shaded spots along our route to the top. Further along, hound's tongue may be found. We then round the mountain and reach the

Summit Bypass Trail. This trail connects to West Cuesta Ridge's "TV Tower Road." Our trail turns hard left and continues another 0.4 mile to

Cerro Alto Summit Trail/West Cuesta Trail. We turn left here and climb 0.3 mile to the summit of Cerro Alto at 2624' for a much-needed rest and sweeping views of San Luis Obispo County. A south view includes Morro Bay, Los Osos, Montaña de Oro, Pismo Dunes, Point Sal, and the Nine Sisters, a chain of volcanic plugs running through Chorro Valley from Morro Bay to San Luis Obispo. A tenth Morro, Davidson Seamount, 3600 feet high, is found in the Pacific Ocean. Its base is 7600 feet below sea level. It is the highest of all the Morros and is the first seamount ever to earn its own name. Leaving the summit we retrace our steps to the

Cerro Alto Summit/West Cuesta Trail Junction. This time we take the left fork and descend to TV Tower Road, passing the Summit bypass trail on the right. At

West Cuesta Ridge Road, we turn right and walk 200 yards to

AT&T Road, again turning right. The trail passes a maintenance shack on the left and the Motor Vehicle Stop. We now start a short but steep descent to a small stream. After crossing the stream, a small hill takes us to the Cerro Alto Campground Trail Junction. Take the left fork and begin a 600-foot descent back to the campground. Along the way the trail contours in and out of small canyons, then enters the forest of bay trees and oaks we left earlier. We eventually come to a bridge over East Morro Creek, a soothing and cool rest spot before the drive home. The trail now swings left, then right, back to Campground Road. The parking lot is visible across the open area to the right.

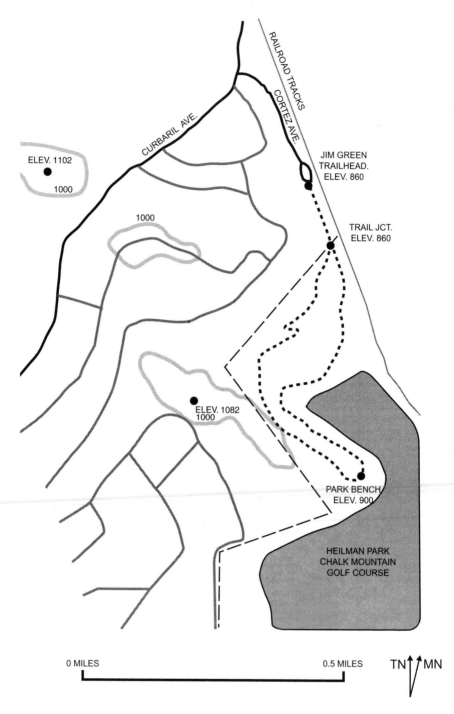

Jim Green

Jim Green

Usage:	Hikers, Horses, Mountain Bikers and Dogs on Leash
Fee:	None
Distance:	1.6 Miles
Elevation Gain/Loss:	120 Feet
Approx. Hiking Time:	1 Hour
Hike Rating:	Easy
USGS Maps:	Atascadero

Best Time to Hike: All Year

Point On Route:	Distance from Starting Point Miles (Km)	Elevation
Jim Green Trailhead	0.0 (0.0)	840
"Y" Intersection	0.1 (0.2)	860
Bench	0.9 (1.4)	960
"Y" Intersection	1.5 (2.4)	860
Jim Green Trailhead	1.6 (2.6)	840

Directions to Trailhead: From San Luis Obispo, allow 20 minutes for the 17.5-mile drive to the trailhead. Take Highway 101 north to Curbaril Ave. in Atascadero. Turn east (right) on Curbaril and drive approximately 0.9 mile to Cortez Ave. Turn right, then drive 0.3 mile to the Jim Green Trail parking area on your left.

Trail Overview: Jim Green is a well-maintained trail along the northern reaches of Heilman Park. It is suitable and fun for all ages. It makes a great evening walk or a cool morning stroll. The trail winds in and out of an oak forest. A bench halfway along the trail overlooks the Chalk Mountain Golf Course. Deer graze in the area in the evenings. In spring, wildflowers can be prolific here as well. For a short trail there is much to see and appreciate.

Trail Description:

Jim Green Trailhead. The trail heads south between two fences along the railroad tracks for a short distance then comes to a

"Y" intersection. Take the right fork. This loop trail returns on the left fork. We head across a field into oak forest. The trail starts a gentle ascent through the forest, reaching two short switchbacks. It climbs over a short rise followed by a short descent, then turns left to head into a canyon before reaching a low saddle. The trail continues almost level through oaks before making a gradual left hand turn and reaching a

bench overlooking the golf course and South Atascadero. This bench makes a convenient stop to take in the view. The trail then descends for a short distance along the golf course. As the hills become steeper, the trail crosses a small creek, then makes a right-hand turn with a gradual ascent to a knoll, again overlooking the golf course. From here, the trail turns left and starts a gradual descent to the "Y" intersection we left earlier. Once at the

"Y" intersection, continue straight along the railroad tracks to return to the

Jim Green Trailhead.

Morro Bay

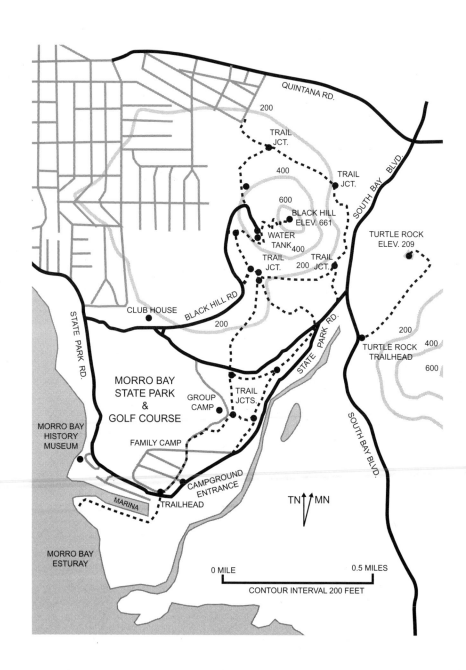

Black Hill/Black Hill Loop

Black Hill

Usage:	Hikers Only
Fee:	None
Distance:	0.6 Miles (Round Trip)
Elevation Gain/Loss:	+200/-200 Feet
Approx. Hiking Time:	1 Hour
Hike Rating:	Easy
USGS Maps:	Morro Bay South

Best Time to Hike: All Year

Point On Route:	Distance from Starting Point Miles(Km)	Elevation
Black Hill Parking Lot	0.0 (0.0)	460
Top of Black Hill	0.3 (0.5)	660
Black Hill Parking Lot	0.6 (1.0)	460

Directions to Trailhead: From San Luis Obispo, drive 12 miles north on Highway 1 to the Los Osos-Baywood Park exit, just before Morro Bay. Turn south onto South Bay Blvd. Drive 0.7 mile to the State Park Entrance. Turn right, then go 0.1 mile to a fork in the road and bear right, up the hill towards the golf course headquarters. Turn right onto the road just before the golf course club house. Drive 0.5 mile to the parking lot near the top of Black Hill.

Trail Overview: This trail is probably the shortest in the guide, but on clear days it offers many photo ops with its great views of Morro Bay, Los Osos, and Chorro Valley. Black Hill, one of the Morros extending from San Luis Obispo to Morro Bay, is dotted with pine trees and wildflowers. At the top you will be treated to views of our magnificent coastline, Cerro Cabrillo, Morro Bay, Hollister Peak, and West Cuesta Ridge.

Trail Description:

Black Hill Parking Lot. The trail starts on the south end of the parking lot, near the water tank. It begins as a slow, gentle climb on a series of switchbacks through chaparral and lush vegetation. Look for wildflowers, including monkey flowers and sage, and remember to stop for a view of Morro Rock through the pines. Continuing our climb, several additional switchbacks take us to the

top of Black Hill at 661 feet, a pleasant, open spot for a rest or a picnic lunch. A variety of birds soar above, including swallows, hawks, turkey vultures and great horned owls. Notice how Morro Rock seems to create its own weather. Clouds form around the Rock while the rest of Morro Bay stays clear. Retrace your steps to the

Black Hill Parking Lot.

BLACK HILL TRAIL

M.F.

Black Hill Loop

Usage:	Hikers Only
Fee:	None
Distance:	1.5 Miles (One Way)
Elevation Gain/Loss:	+660/-660 Feet
Approx. Hiking Time:	1 - 2 Hours
Hike Rating:	Moderate
USGS Maps:	Morro Bay South

Best Time to Hike: All Year

Point On Route:	Distance from Starting Point Miles(Km)	Elevation
Campground Entrance	0.0 (0.0)	20
Exercise Trail	0.3 (0.0)	80
Black Hill Road	0.5 (0.8)	160
Trail Junction 1	0.9(1.4)	240
Trail Junction 2	0.9 (1.4)	260
"T" Junction	1.1 (1.9)	420
Water Tank	1.2 (2.0)	480
Junction to Parking Lot	1.2 (2.0)	480
Black Hill Summit	1.5 (2.4)	660

Directions to Trailhead: From San Luis Obispo, drive 12 miles north on Highway 1 to the Los Osos-Baywood Park exit, just before Morro Bay. Turn south onto South Bay Boulevard. Drive 0.7 mile to State Park Road, then turn right. Go another 0.1 mile, then bear left 0.7 mile to the campground entrance. Park in the parking area just beyond the campground entrance, adjacent to the bathrooms.

Trail Overview: Black Hill is one of the Morros, the series of peaks extending from Morro Rock to Islay Hill in San Luis Obispo. The trail ascends from just above sea level through coastal scrub, chaparral, eucalyptus, oak woodland and pines, to the summit, 660 feet above sea level. Great views of Morro Bay, Chorro Valley and the estuary can be seen from the top. One might also see cliff swallows, hawks, and turkey vultures soaring overhead.

Trail Description:

Campground Entrance. Walk back 200 feet to the campground entrance. Take the road to the right, under the pines, to the picnic area, then up towards the Group Camp Area. Just before you reach the group camp the

Exercise Trail is reached. Turn right onto the Exercise Trail and follow it around a large pine. The trail then swings to the left, skirting the Group Camps. The trail may be faint at times, but it gets distinct when it reaches another junction on the Exercise Trail. At this junction continue left up the hill through chaparral, passing another junction. Immediately beyond this junction may be a sign pointing you towards Black Hill. In a short distance, you now reach the

Road leading to the Black Hill Golf Course Headquarters. The trail continues across the road through vegetation thick with many flowers. Another junction, apparently an old road, is reached shortly. Turn left up the hill across bare roots to yet another

Junction. These two junctions can be used to make a couple of longer loops on the descent from Black Hill. Keep left to another junction and turn right here, climbing more steeply now as we parallel Black Hill Road. To make for a more pleasant hike, the road is hidden from view. Along this route there are several more side trails leading to the road itself. Continue straight up the hill. Eventually you will reach what appears to be a

"T" junction. The left trail is fainter and connects to Black Hill Road. We turn right and ascend Black Hill around a huge water tank. Just beyond the water tank is the

Junction to the parking lot. Continue straight, climbing ¼ mile and traversing 6 switchbacks to the summit of

Black Hill.

Return Trip

Two options are available for a semiloop trip back to the campground.

The first is a 1.1 mile trail that skirts the southern edge of Black Hill, then returns along State Park Road, intersecting with the Exercise Trail. From the **Junction** described above take this trail around the south west side of Black Hill to a "T" intersection overlooking South Bay Blvd. Turn right here, then descend to State Park Road. Turn right, then follow the road to the "Y" intersection. Immediately past the intersection on the left the trail can be found under a large pine tree. Follow this trail to the Exercise Trail. Take the left fork of the Exercise Trail back to the group camps. Now retrace your steps to the Campground Entrance.

The second trail is much shorter, a direct route down Black Hill. This trail follows what appears to be the old road, which connects directly to the trail at the "Y" intersection, rejoining the Exercise Trail as well. See the map of the area for route information.

MORRO BAY from BLACK HILL

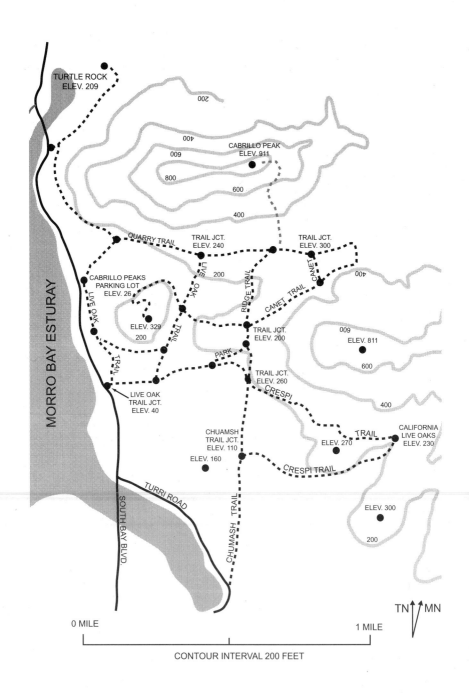

TURTLE ROCK
ELEV. 209

200

400

600

CABRILLO PEAK
ELEV. 911

800

600

400

QUARRY TRAIL

TRAIL JCT.
ELEV. 240

TRAIL JCT.
ELEV. 300

CABRILLO PEAKS
PARKING LOT
ELEV. 26

LIVE OAK

200

LIVE OAK

RIDGE TRAIL

CANET TRAIL

CANET

400

ELEV. 329

200

TRAIL

PARK

TRAIL JCT.
ELEV. 200

600

ELEV. 811

600

MORRO BAY ESTURAY

TRAIL

LIVE OAK
TRAIL JCT.
ELEV. 40

TRAIL JCT.
ELEV. 260

CRESPI

400

CALIFORNIA
LIVE OAKS
ELEV. 230

CHUAMSH
TRAIL JCT.
ELEV. 110

ELEV. 160

TRAIL

ELEV. 270

CRESPI TRAIL

TURRI ROAD

SOUTH BAY BLVD.

CHUMASH TRAIL

ELEV. 300

200

TN ↑ ↑ MN

0 MILE

1 MILE

CONTOUR INTERVAL 200 FEET

Cabrillo Peaks Loop

Cabrillo Peaks Loop

Usage:	Hikers, Mountain Bikers and Horses
Fee:	None
Distance:	4.2 Miles (Round Trip)
Elevation Gain/Loss:	+600/-600 Feet
Approx. Hiking Time:	2-3 Hours
Hike Rating:	Moderate
USGS Maps:	Morro Bay South

Best Time to Hike: All Year

Point On Route:	Distance from Starting Point Miles(Km)	Elevation
Cabrillo Peaks Parking Lot	0.0 (0.0)	26
Live Oak Trail	0.5 (0.8)	240
Canet Trail	0.9 (1.4)	300
Junction Park Ridge Trail	1.3 (2.1)	260
Crespi Trail	1.5 (2.4)	200
California Live Oaks	2.3 (3.4)	230
Chumash Trail	3.0 (4.5)	110
Crespi Trail	3.3 (5.0)	200
Live Oak Trail	3.8 (5.8)	40
Cabrillo Peaks Parking Lot	4.2 (6.4)	26

Directions to Trailhead: From San Luis Obispo, drive 12 miles north on Highway 1 to the Los Osos-Baywood Park exit, just before Morro Bay. Turn south onto South Bay Boulevard. Drive 0.7 mile to the State Park Entrance. Continue straight for 0.2 miles and look for the dirt parking lot on the left. It is easy to miss.

Trail Overview: Cabrillo Peaks Area is the newest addition to Morro Bay State Park. It offers a wide selection of trails and views of Cabrillo Peaks, the backside of Hollister Peak, the Morro Bay Estuary, and expansive grasslands. Wildflowers thrive here during spring and summer months. You may find a few ticks and possibly poison oak as well. The rolling hills of this area are great for hiking, cycling, or horseback riding. We describe one trail here, but other trips are available. We encourage everyone to explore this beautiful area.

Trail Description:

Cabrillo Peaks Parking Lot. The trail starts on the northeast end of the parking lot on the Quarry Trail. It begins with a gentle grade, quickly reaching the Turtle Rock trail junction to the left. Continue straight, climbing up the old quarry road. Cabrillo Peak is on our left. The trail levels out to reach the

Live Oak Trail Junction. Follow the Quarry Trail past a few other trails on the left, one of which takes you to the base of Cabrillo Peak. A trail to the top is in the works. On the right you will find the Park Ridge Trail, immediately followed by the

Canet Trail. Turn right onto the Canet Trail. The trail straight ahead leads you to the park boundary and an unnamed, slightly longer, and much steeper trail which rejoins the Canet Trail. Our route heads south on a gradual ascent to meet the unnamed trail entering from the left. Climbing a bit more, we then start a gentle descent to reach the

Park Ridge Trail. Turn left onto the Park Ridge Trail. The Chumash Trail is a short distance ahead. Stay to the left, cross a seep, then come to the Crespi Trail Junction. Continuing to the left, we hike to the other reaches of Cabrillo Peak Area behind Hollister Peak. The trail remains level here. A couple of trails take off the left side. Continue straight on the Crespi Trail. We come to a saddle overlooking a small valley to start a gentle descent to a grove of

Coast Live Oaks. The trail makes a 180-degree turn here, crossing a small creek, which it follows downstream for a short distance, then crosses again. The trail then climbs 100 feet to the ridge above. Once on top of the ridge, we can see the entire Morro Bay Estuary, Turri Road, Los Osos and Baywood. Black Hill and Cabrillo Peaks are due north, Hollister Peak east from our location. The trail winds right, then left, descending to the

Chumash Trail. Turn right, climbing back to the

Crespi Trail junction. Turn left again, staying on the Crespi Trail all the way to the Southern Cabrillo Peaks Entrance. Once at the entrance we take the

Live Oak Trail on the right (north). We skirt the hillside, following South Bay Boulevard to the northern side of the Cabrillo Peaks Area to return to our starting point,

Cabrillo Peaks Parking Lot.

From Black Hill Trail

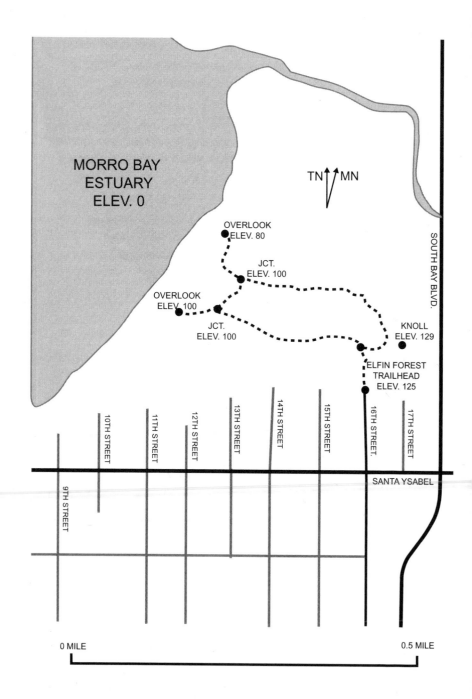

Elfin Forest

Elfin Forest

Usage:	Hikers, Wheel Chair Accessible
Fee:	None
Distance:	1.5 Miles
Elevation Gain/Loss:	+70/ -70 Feet
Approx. Hiking Time:	1 – 2 Hours
Hike Rating:	Easy
USGS Maps:	Morro Bay South

Best Time to Hike: All Year

Directions to Trailhead: Take Highway 1 to the South Bay Boulevard exit in Morro Bay. Head south towards Los Osos. Turn right onto Santa Ysabel Street. Turn right again onto 16th Street and park in the parking area at the end of the street. If the parking lot is full and you must park in the street, please make sure not to block any driveways.

Trail Overview: The Elfin Forest was purchased by the County of San Luis Obispo several years ago and is now open to the public. A 1.5 mile board-walk was built by the CCC (California Conservation Corps) to protect the fragile habitat and make the area wheelchair accessible. Along this board-walk, one can enjoy the estuary with its natural offerings: coastal dune scrub, morro manzanita and a host of wildlife species. The wind-swept, gnarled, 500-year-old pygmy oaks are a special sight. Who knows what else you might encounter along this trail?

Trail Description:

The boardwalk begins through dense coastal sage on both sides. Reaching the ridge trail, we turn left (west) towards the Morro Bay Estuary. The highest points of the Elfin Forest offer good views of the estuary and Morro Bay State Park. In a short distance, we come to the Celestial Meadow Trail Junction. Continue past this junction to the first of three viewing platforms from which one can enjoy the view. Retracing your path to the Celestial Meadow Junction, turn left (north) to continue along the boardwalk to the next junction. The left path takes you to the second overlook closer to the bay. We will continue straight, deeper into Elfin Forest. Along this path a jumping-off point is possible to explore the Pygmy Oaks themselves and imagine what it might be like to be a dwarf scurrying under the trees. They make neat forts, as you will see. The boardwalk continues east, gets closer to South Bay Boulevard, and offers views of the Cabrillo Peaks Area. We then start a short climb to the Ridge Trail Junction. Turning left takes the hiker to the third platform, where Turri Road and the backside of Hollister Peak come into view. Leaving the viewing area, we follow the ridge trail back to the 16th Street junction, where a left turn brings us back to the parking lot.

Los Osos Oaks State Reserve

Usage:	Hikers
Fee:	None
Distance:	1-2 Miles
Elevation Gain/Loss:	+100/-100 Feet
Approx. Hiking Time:	1 – 2 Hours
Hike Rating:	Easy
USGS Maps:	Morro Bay South

Best Time to Hike: All Year

Directions to Trailhead: From San Luis Obispo, take Los Osos Valley Road towards Los Osos. Continue past Turri Road about 2 miles. Just past Los Osos Creek, at the base of a small hill, look for a parking lot and sign indicating the Los Osos Oaks State Reserve. If you get to South Bay Boulevard you have gone too far.

From Morro Bay, take 101 South to the South Bay Boulevard exit. Take South Bay Boulevard to Los Osos Valley Road in Los Osos and turn left. Continue for 0.7 mile and watch for the parking lot on the right.

Trail Overview: The Los Osos Oaks State Reserve is an 85-acre reserve created in 1971 thanks to a donation from Dart Industries. This reserve contains ancient dwarf oaks, some as old as 800 years. Over the centuries, they have twisted and turned into gnarled shapes. Lace lichen has made its home on the oaks. Take your time to explore this mystical place. A variety of wildflowers is present most of the year. Beware of poison oak, especially if you get off the main trails.

Trail Description:

Leaving the parking lot, we cross a wooden bridge, then reach a junction of three different trails. These will loop towards each other on the other end. They are the Los Osos Creek, Oak View, and Chumash Loop trails respectively. We recommend taking the Oak View trail and returning on either the Chumash or Los Osos Creek trails. On the relatively wide Oak View Trail, we will wander through a wonderful gnarled forest of dwarf oaks. Their limbs have grown to measure between 25 and 50 feet in length, eventually touching the ground for support. This dense forest creates such deep shade that few plants are able to grow under the oaks.

At the next trail junction we have three choices: to return via the Chumash Loop Trail, to return via the Los Osos Creek Trail, or to continue straight ahead on the Oak View Trail. We recommend the third option. The trail continues through oaks, then swings left to a "T" intersection in a grassy meadow. The trails to the right allow the hiker to explore the reserve, but they all come to a dead end. Turn left at the "T" and hike through an open grassland/chaparral area. Check the views of Los Osos Valley, the Santa Lucia Range, and the Morros. We quickly reach another trail junction. The left trail returns to the Oak View and Chumash Loop Trails, but we continue straight, winding in and out of lush vegetation and wildflowers, including blue-eyed grass and hummingbird sage. A few side trails lead to overlooks of Los Osos Creek. If you wish to explore the overlooks, be careful on the steep cliffs. Los Osos Valley Road comes into view as the trail turns west to return to our starting point, the entrance to Los Osos Oaks State Reserve.

Sweet Springs Nature Preserve

Usage:	Hikers
Fee:	None
Distance:	0.5 to 1 Mile
Elevation Gain/Loss:	+50/-50 Feet
Approx. Hiking Time:	1 Hour
Hike Rating:	Easy
USGS Maps:	Morro Bay South

Best Time to Hike: All Year

Directions to Trailhead: From San Luis Obispo, take Los Osos Valley Road to Los Osos. Drive straight through Los Osos toward Montaña de Oro State Park. Approximately 0.5 mile past South Bay Boulevard, just before Monarch Grove Elementary School, turn right on Pine Street and then right on Broderson Street at the "T" intersection. The Nature Preserve will be on your left.

From Morro Bay, take 101 South to the South Bay Boulevard exit. Continue on South Bay Boulevard to Los Osos Valley Road. Turn right, then follow the directions above to reach the Nature Preserve.

Trail Overview: Sweet Springs Nature Preserve is a 24-acre wetland, home to the Belted Kingfisher. It also provides a haven to many other birds, turtles, monarch butterflies and other creatures of the Morro Bay Estuary. This wetland area offers great views of the Morro Bay Estuary. It is maintained mostly by local volunteers, who have traditionally worked the second Saturday of each month to maintain the trails and restore the natural habitat.

Trail Description:

As we walk through the gate, the trail enters a large eucalyptus grove with a pond visible below. A trail comes in from the right. Continue straight to one of two wooden bridges. As you cross the bridge, look for turtles or other pond wildlife. At the junction just past the bridge, turn left to stroll out over another bridge, then along the eucalyptus grove to the west end of the Preserve and a "T" intersection. The trail to the left returns to Broderson Street. The right trail takes you to a bench on the edge of the Estuary, a great place to read a book and observe wildlife. This portion of the trail can be boggy in wet weather as well as high tides.

Before you leave this beautiful spot, you may want to take the trail we saw near the first bridge and walk around the eastern edge of the pond.

Santa Margarita Lake

Grey Pine
Rocky Point
Blinn
Sandstone

CABRILLO PEAK AREA

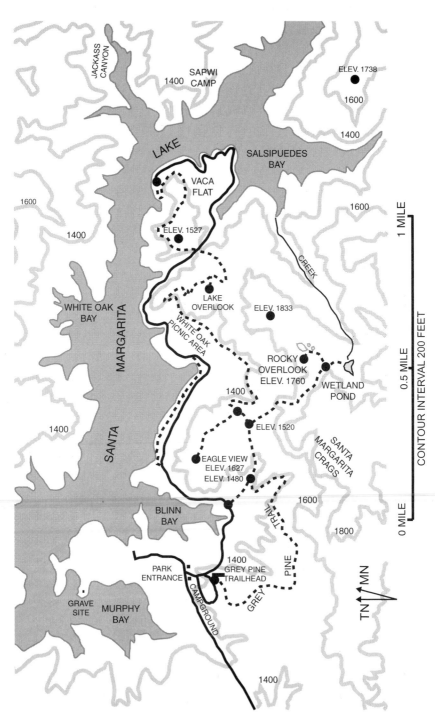

Santa Margarita Lake

Grey Pine – Vaca Flat Loop

Usage:	Hikers, Horses and Dogs on Leash
Fee:	Santa Margarita Lake Park Entrance Day Use Fee
Distance:	5.9 Miles Round Trip (7.2 Miles with Side Trips)
Elevation Gain/Loss:	+800/ -800 Feet
Approx. Hiking Time:	4 Hours
Hike Rating:	Moderate
USGS Maps:	Santa Margarita Lake

Best Time to Hike: Winter, Spring, Fall, Summer Evenings

Point On Route:	Distance from Starting Point Miles(Km)	Elevation
Grey Pine Trailhead	0.0 (0.0)	1420
Trail Junction	1.0 (1.6)	1480
Santa Margarita Crags Trail Junction	1.3 (2.1)	1560
Eagle View Trail Junction	1.3 (2.1)	1560
White Oak Flat	1.9 (3.0)	1360
Vaca Flat Road	2.7 (4.3)	1440
Vaca Flat	3.5 (5.6)	1360
White Oak Flat	4.5 (7.2)	1360
Main Road	5.1 (8.2)	1380
Grey Pine Campground	5.6 (9.0)	1420

Directions to Trailhead: From Hwy 101, take the Santa Margarita (Highway 58) exit and turn east toward Santa Margarita. Turn right on Highway 58. At the junction with Pozo Road and Highway 58, follow the signs to Santa Margarita Lake (Pozo Road). Drive approximately 7 miles to the Santa Margarita Lake turnoff. Turn left and drive one mile to the Santa Margarita Lake County Park Entrance. Turn right after entering the gate and park in the Grey Pine Campground parking area immediately to the right of the entrance to the park. The Grey Pine Trail is 100 yards across from the campground.

Trail Overview: This loop trail wanders through gently rolling hills, grasslands and the oak-studded canyons of Santa Margarita Lake County Park. It offers close-up views of the Santa Margarita Crags, home to many bird species including eagles and peregrine falcons. Winter and spring wildflowers along the trail include shooting stars, red maids, California buttercups and hummingbird sage. Most of the trail described is shared with horses. The views from the overlooks are spectacular. This trail may be too hot during the day in the summer months, but it makes a wonderful evening walk. It is fairly clear of poison oak.

Trail Description:

Grey Pine Trailhead. The trail skirts the campground and heads into the oak woodland around the lake. In a short while we can see Blinn Bay, one of many views of Santa Margarita Lake. The trail continues to wander in and out of several small canyons, with a variety of wildflowers, lichens and unique rock formations. At the one-mile point we come to a

Trail Junction. The left fork returns to Grey Pine Campground. The right fork continues toward White Oak Flat. We take this fork 0.3 mile to the

Santa Margarita Crags Trail Junction. Turn right and climb 250 feet in 0.4 mile to the ridge. At the ridge we find a trail junction. The left fork leads to a rocky outcropping overlooking Santa Margarita Lake. The right fork goes to a natural wetland pond high above the lake. Retrace your steps to the Santa Margarita Crags Trail Junction. Our journey continues towards White Oak Flat. Within 100 feet we come to the Eagle View Trail, a short 0.2-mile trip one way, for a lake overlook. We take the right fork traveling to 0.6 mile to

White Oak Flat, improved with bathroom, picnic area and boat ramp. Leaving White Oak Flat we start a moderate 250' climb over the ridge. Along this trail we find a bench with views of Santa Margarita Lake. The summit offers views of the backcountry behind the lake. These include the narrows, Sapwi backpackers' and boaters' camp, and the rugged mountains on the northside of the lake. The trail now descends to

Vaca Flat Road. Crossing the road, the trail continues toward Vaca Flat. Look for a rocky outcropping on the left, which makes a good lunch spot. Another 0.6 mile takes us to

Vaca Flat. From the north end of Vaca Flat follow the level dirt road. Note the views of Salsipuedes Bay. We go around Vaca Flat over a small saddle until we return to

White Oak Flat. Take the dirt road on the right just past White Oak Flat, again at lake level until it reaches the main road. Continue on the main road over our last hill to park headquarters and back to the starting point at

Grey Pine Campground.

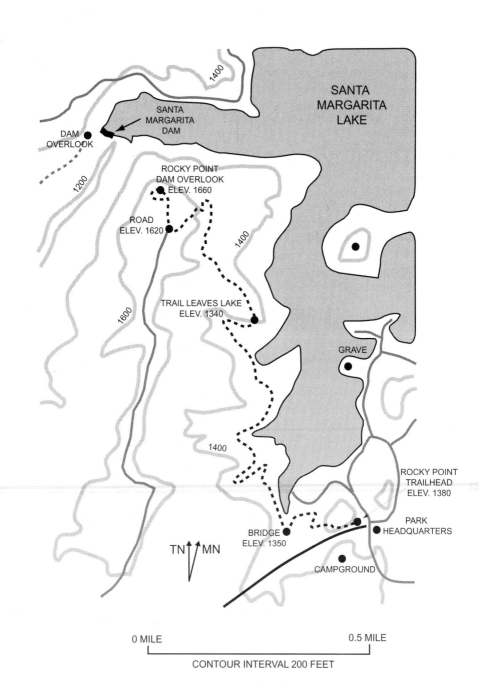

SANTA MARGARITA LAKE

SANTA MARGARITA DAM

DAM OVERLOOK

1400

1200

ROCKY POINT DAM OVERLOOK ELEV. 1660

ROAD ELEV. 1620

1600

1400

TRAIL LEAVES LAKE ELEV. 1340

GRAVE

1400

ROCKY POINT TRAILHEAD ELEV. 1380

PARK HEADQUARTERS

TN MN

BRIDGE ELEV. 1350

CAMPGROUND

0 MILE

0.5 MILE

CONTOUR INTERVAL 200 FEET

Rocky Point

Rocky Point

Usage:	Hikers, Horses, Mountain Bikers and Dogs on Leash
Fee:	Santa Margarita Lake Park Entrance Day Use Fee
Distance:	1.8 Miles (One Way)
Elevation Gain/Loss:	+450/ -200 Feet
Approx. Hiking Time:	2-3 Hours
Hike Rating:	Moderate
USGS Maps:	Santa Margarita Lake

Best Time to Hike: Winter, Spring, Fall, Summer Evenings

Point On Route:	Distance from Starting Point Miles(Km)	Elevation
Rocky Point Trailhead	0.0 (0.0)	1380
Bridge	0.2 (0.3)	1350
Trail leaves shore	1.0 (1.6)	1340
Road	1.7 (2.7)	1620
Rocky Point	1.8 (2.9)	1660

Directions to Trailhead: From U.S. 101, take the Santa Margarita exit and drive east toward Santa Margarita. Turn right on Highway 58. At the junction with Pozo Road, follow the signs to Santa Margarita Lake (Pozo Road). Drive approximately 7 miles to the Santa Margarita Lake turnoff. Turn left and drive 1 mile to the Santa Margarita Lake County Park Entrance. Turn right after entering the gate and park in the Grey Pine Campground parking area immediately to the right of the entrance to the park. The Rocky Point Trail is across the street from the park entrance on the west side of the road.

Trail Overview: This trail explores the southern and western edges of Santa Margarita Lake as it winds in and out through oak studded forest, grey pines, grasslands and chaparral. There are many winter and spring wildflowers along the trail, including shooting stars, red maids, California buttercups, mariposa lilies, larkspur, gentian, woolly blue curls and hummingbird sage. The trail is named after Hans "Rocky" Thiel, a long time park ranger at Santa Margarita Lake, now retired. The trail itself was built by a volunteer effort encompassing the Sierra Club, Central Coast Concerned Mountain Bikers (CCCMB), and horse riders' organizations. This two-mile section of trail is part of a 25-mile loop that is currently under construction around Santa Margarita Lake. This trail may be too hot during the day in the summer months, but it makes a wonderful evening walk. It is fairly clear of poison oak.

Trail Description:

Rocky Point Trailhead. The trail follows the fence line for a short distance, with views of Santa Margarita Crags, then descends down a hillside on a short switchback to reach a

bridge on one of Lake Santa Margarita's many tributaries. Once across the tributary, the trail is level for the next 0.8 mile, following the edge of the lake and winding in and out of many small inlets. Grey pines and oaks are abundant here. You may even see a deer or fox. Reaching the far end of the lake the

trail leaves the shore, starting a gradual climb up the hillside through many small canyons. The grassy areas give way to thick chaparral. After climbing 300 feet, the trail hits the ridge top on a

dirt road. Go to the right towards the end of the road. Please do not go left as you will shortly cross onto private property. At the end of the

road you will be high above the lake on Rocky Point Overlook with 360-degree views. Below is the Santa Margarita Dam. This trail will eventually be extended, allowing you to cross the Salinas River and continue around the lake.

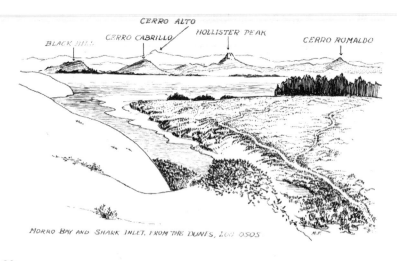

MORRO BAY AND SHARK INLET, FROM THE DUNES, LOS OSOS

CAMBRIA, FISCALINI RANCH

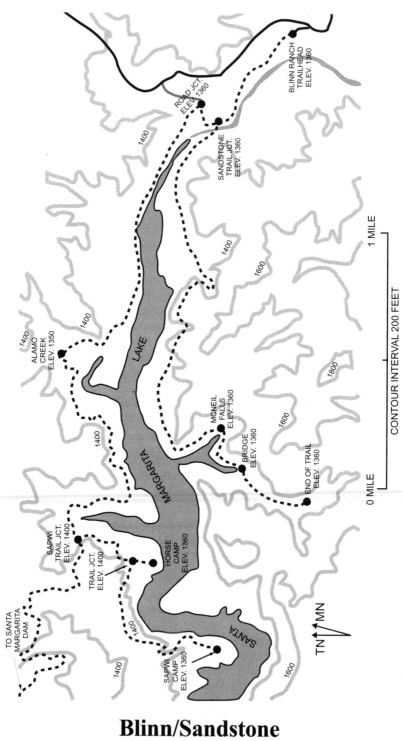

Blinn/Sandstone

Blinn Ranch

Usage:	Hikers, Horses, Mountain Bikes and Dogs on Leash
Fee:	Santa Margarita Lake Park Entrance Day Use Fee
Distance:	9.2 Miles (Round Trip)
Elevation Gain/Loss:	+600/-600 Feet
Approx. Hiking Time:	4-6 Hours
Hike Rating:	Moderate
USGS Maps:	Santa Margarita Lake

Best Time to Hike: Winter, Spring, Fall, Summer Evenings

Point On Route:	Distance from Starting Point Miles(Km)	Elevation
Blinn Ranch Trailhead	0.0 (0.0)	1360
Sandstone Trail Junction	0.5 (0.8)	1360
Alamo Creek	1.9 (3.0)	1320
Sapwi Trail Junction	3.2 (5.2)	1400
Horse Camp Junction	3.6 (5.8)	1400
Sapwi Camp	4.6 (7.4)	1360

Directions to Trailhead: From Hwy. 101, take the Santa Margarita exit and drive east toward Santa Margarita. Turn right on Highway 58. At the junction with Pozo Road and Highway 58, follow the signs to Santa Margarita Lake (Pozo Road). Drive approximately 7 miles to the Santa Margarita Lake turnoff. Continue on Pozo Road another 8 miles to River Road Junction. Turn left and drive 2.2 miles to the River Road entrance of Santa Margarita Lake.

Trail Overview: The Sapwi (Indian for "deer") Camp Trail explores the northern side of Santa Margarita Lake. Mainly an access road to the dam, this trail offers good footing and a fairly level walk, sandy in places. Many oaks and pines provide welcome shade on a hot day. If you have made arrangements in advance, you may stay overnight at Sapwi Camp. The camp may also be reached by boat from White Oak Flat launch area on the south side of Santa Margarita Lake.

Trail Description:

Blinn Ranch Trailhead. The trail starts on the north side of the parking area. We walk through a swing gate onto an old road, which is paved at some point. This area can be boggy in wet weather. Wild roses grow on both sides of the road. Continuing, the trail passes by oaks to a junction with

Sandstone Trail. Our trail turns right here. Several large sandstone rocks on our left are worth a closer look. Wind and rain have eroded the rocks, creating many holes and small caves. Our trail comes to Toro Creek, which runs most of the year, forded by a makeshift bridge to the left. We reach another road where we turn left. Follow the road along the Salinas River, through a gate, to the back end of Santa Margarita Lake. The road eventually starts a gentle climb over a small knoll, then descends to

Alamo Creek. From here the trail continues to undulate over several small ridges, dipping in and out of canyons along the lake. Look for fresh water clam shells, the remnants of a raccoon dinner. This side of the lake is covered with many oaks and grey pines. After 2.8 miles, the trail starts a fairly steep ascent. Luckily, we only have to climb a short distance before we reach the

Sapwi Trail Junction. If you want to hike to the Santa Margarita Dam, continue along the road for another three to five miles. Our trail turns left here. The trail is fairly level and gets easier as we approach the lake. We now come to the Horse Camp Junction. The trail straight ahead leads to the horse camp. The right trail continues to our destination, Sapwi Camp. The trail is surrounded on both sides by chamise at first, then starts to open up as it gets closer to the camp. We stay about 100 feet above the lake with nice views of the Santa Margarita Narrows below. Eventually, the trail starts to cross an open meadow with the lake on the left. The trail may be quite narrow here as it gets closer to the lake. When you reach

Sapwi Camp, you will find pit toilets, six campsites and a large fire ring, as well as a dock 100 yards beyond the camp. The point to the left of the dock makes a good lunch spot.

Sandstone

Usage:	Hikers, Horses, Mtn. Bikes and Dogs on Leash
Fee:	Santa Margarita Lake Park Entrance Day Use Fee
Distance:	2.7 Miles (One Way)
Elevation Gain/Loss:	+200/-200 Feet
Approx. Hiking Time:	2-3 Hours
Hike Rating:	Moderate
USGS Maps:	Santa Margarita Lake

Best Time to Hike: Winter, Spring, Fall, Summer Evenings

Point On Route:	Distance from Starting Point Miles (Km)	Elevation
Blinn Ranch Trailhead	0.0 (0.0)	1360
Sandstone Trail Junction	0.5 (0.8)	1360
McNeil Canyon	2.0 (3.2)	1360
End of Trail	2.7 (4.3)	1360

Directions to Trailhead: From Hwy 101, take the Santa Margarita (Highway 58) exit and drive east toward Santa Margarita. Turn right on Highway 58. At the junction with Pozo Road and Highway 58, follow the signs to Santa Margarita Lake (Pozo Road). Drive approximately 7 miles to the Santa Margarita Lake turnoff. Continue on Pozo Road another 8 miles to River Road Junction. Turn left and drive 2.2 miles to the River Road entrance of Santa Margarita Lake.

Trail Overview: This trail is mainly an old dirt road. It starts at the bâck end of Santa Margarita Lake Park and explores the Salinas River and the southeast end of Santa Margarita Lake. There are many views of the lake itself, and in the winter months McNeil Falls adds a nice highlight to the trip. As with all trails at Santa Margarita Lake, there are abundant wildflowers for most of the year.

Trail Description:

Blinn Ranch Trailhead. The trail starts on the north side of the parking area. We walk through a swing gate onto an old road, probably paved at one point. This area can be boggy in wet weather. Wild roses and snowberries grow on both sides of the road. Continuing, the trail passes by oaks to a junction with the

Sandstone Trail. The Blinn Ranch Trail goes to the right. Continue straight, crossing the Salinas River. Depending on the time of the year, one's feet may get wet, and the crossing may be hazardous. Running water is deeper than it appears. For your own safety, do not cross the river if you are at all unsure. Once across, the trail follows an old road which has narrowed into a well-defined path. At the one-mile mark the trail enters a forested canyon, then winds it way to the top of a open ridge which offers great views of Santa Margarita Lake. We then descend back to the lake, then swing left into

McNeil Canyon. The trail winds around the inlet to McNeil Falls, which tumbles 40 feet over a sandstone cliff. Past the falls the trail comes to a concrete bridge, then continues ¼ mile to a locked gate in a forested canyon. This is the

end of the trail. This trail will eventually connect to the west side of the lake as part of a 25-mile loop currently being constructed at Santa Margarita Lake.

Montaña de Oro

SPOONER'S COVE

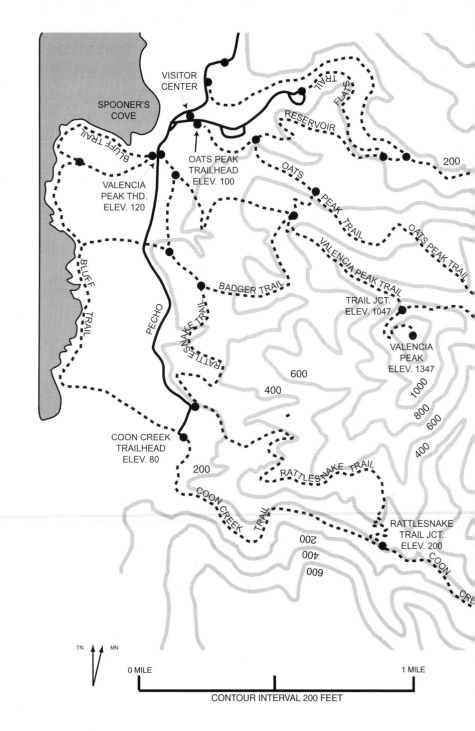

Montaña de Oro South

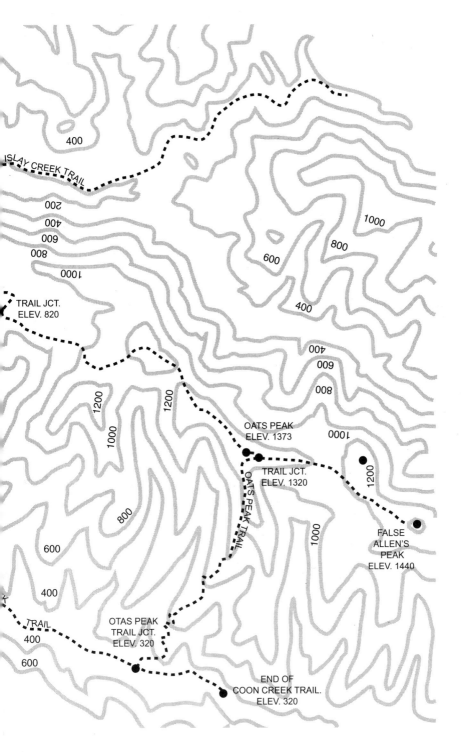

ISLAY CREEK TRAIL

400

200
400
600
800
1000

TRAIL JCT.
ELEV. 820

1200

1200

1000

800

600

400

TRAIL

400

600

OTAS PEAK
TRAIL JCT.
ELEV. 320

OATS PEAK TRAIL

OATS PEAK
ELEV. 1373

TRAIL JCT.
ELEV. 1320

1000

600

800

400

600

800

1000

1200

FALSE
ALLEN'S
PEAK
ELEV. 1440

1000

END OF
COON CREEK TRAIL.
ELEV. 320

Montaña de Oro Bluff

Usage:	Hikers and Mountain Bikers
Fee:	None at this Time
Distance:	2.1 Miles One Way
Elevation Gain/Loss:	+100/-100 Feet
Approx. Hiking Time:	1-3 Hours
Hike Rating:	Easy
USGS Maps:	Morro Bay South

Best Time to Hike: All Year

Point On Route:	Distance from Starting Point Miles(Km)	Elevation
Bluff Trailhead	0.0 (0.0)	120
Corallina Cove	0.6 (1.0)	40
Quarry Cove	1.1 (1.7)	40
Grotto Rock	1.7 (2.7)	40
Pecho Road	2.1 (3.4)	80

Directions to Trailhead: From San Luis Obispo take Los Osos Valley Road through Los Osos, then continue on to the entrance of Montaña de Oro State Park via Pecho Valley Road. Drive another 2.7 miles to Park Headquarters Visitor Center (also known as Old Ranch House). The trailhead is located 400 feet beyond, on the south side of Spooner's Cove.

Trail Overview: This trail, the most popular in Montaña de Oro State Park, follows an alluvial terrace overlooking a series of rugged cliffs. The bluff is peppered with signs warning, "Danger/Sheer cliff/Stay back." The trail features a series of dramatic views of rock carved by crashing surf. Harbor seals frequent the shore. In winter, gray whales may be sighted. In summer, pigeon guillemots build nests in holes in the cliffs at the south end of the bluff. Other birds found in the area include cormorants, gulls, and pelicans. Many rodents scurry among the matted grasses of the sea terraces. In spring the entire area is covered by masses of colorful wildflowers, including mustard, wild radish, locoweed, coast golden yarrow, and California poppy. New Zealand spinach borders most of the trail. Because of the hazardous cliffs, hikers with children should be especially cautious. Beware of poison oak, especially in the first portion of the trail.

Trail Description:

Bluff Trailhead starts about 500 feet south of Park Headquarters on the west side of the road. We start by crossing a wooden bridge over an intermittent creek. The trail climbs a small rise to views of a smaller cove, known as Smugglers' Cove. There used to be a tunnel chute to an old pier here for loading goods from the Pecho Ranch in the late 1800's to early 1900's. During Prohibition it was a transfer point for contraband whiskey. The trail continues along the south side of Spooner's Cove with Morro Rock in the distance to the north. Seals may be spotted in the surf. We now turn left and begin to head south. On the second point there is a blowhole, active during high tide. Just past the blowhole we come to a trail junction. The right fork takes you down a series of steps to

Corallina Cove. This is a great place to explore tide pools. The cove is named after coralline algae, not coral reefs. Watch for seals and sea otters among the kelp, and look for piddock clam holes in many of the rocks. We continue to the left to a wooden bridge. Cross the bridge, then turn immediately to the right to gain another view of Corallina Cove. We continue following the trail south along the bluff. On your left is a wide-open field, and on the right, many small coves resembling bowling alleys. At high tide, these alleyways fill with froth. The trail starts a swinging left turn as it parallels

Quarry Cove. The large amounts of open terrain covered with shale give this cove its name. Just past Quarry Cove we come to another junction. The trail to the left goes to Pecho Road. Take the right fork and continue on to a unique castle-type rock formation. This is a hollow formation where waves can be seen rushing in and out under the rock itself. Just past this point we come to

Grotto Rock. Most people stop here as the 0.3 mile trail to

Pecho Road is uneventful. If you desire, you can retrace your steps or follow Pecho Road back to your starting point. This loop trail is a total of 3.7 miles.

COON CREEK
TRAIL

M. FOSTER

Coon Creek

Usage:	Hikers and Horses
Fee:	None at this Time
Distance:	2.5 Miles (One Way)
Elevation Gain/Loss:	240 Feet
Approx. Hiking Time:	2-4 Hours
Hike Rating:	Easy to Moderate
USGS Maps:	Morro Bay South

Best Time to Hike: All Year

Point On Route:	Distance from Starting Point Miles(Km)	Elevation
Coon Creek Trailhead	0.0 (0.0)	80
First Bridge	0.4 (0.7)	140
Second Bridge	0.7 (1.2)	140
Rattlesnake Flats Trail Jct.	1.0 (1.7)	200
Oats Peak Trail	2.3 (3.7)	320
Cypress Grove	2.5 (4.0)	320

Directions to Trailhead: From San Luis Obispo take Los Osos Valley Road to Los Osos, then continue on to the entrance of Montaña de Oro State Park via Pecho Valley Road. Drive another 2.7 miles to Park Headquarters (Visitor Center, or Old Ranch House). The trailhead is located 400 feet east of the Park Headquarters on the south side of the campground.

Trail Overview: Coon Creek is one of the easier trails in the park. It climbs only 300 feet for the 2.5-mile journey to the cypress grove. There are several bridges crossing a year-round stream as you wind your way through the canyon. Look for trout fry darting in the stream. Wildflowers are abundant most of the year, including honeysuckle, sage, trillium, false Solomon's seal, and monkey flowers. High on the hills to the south you can see one of the few stands of Bishop pines in the area. There are large stands of live oaks, willows, and coffeeberry along the route. Watch for poison oak and stinging nettle along the trail. Ticks are present most of the year.

Trail Description:

Coon Creek Trailhead. Our trail starts at the end of Pecho Road and quickly descends into Coon Creek Canyon. The year-round stream is on our right but is hard to see through the thick vegetation. We cross the

first bridge, one of six along this route. On the south side of the creek we encounter dense vegetation on all sides and sometimes above us. You will find many different plant species along this route. We now come to the

second bridge. This is the easiest access point to Coon Creek itself. There is a large section of rocky beach adjacent to the creek. If you look closely here you may see small fish hiding in the streambed. The trail climbs slightly above the streambed onto a rocky shale cliff. You may see a chert outcropping on your right and a view of the Bishop pines on the ridge to the south. We pass a small cave on the left about 50 feet above the trail, then come to the

Rattlesnake Flats Trail junction. From here to the cypress grove you may encounter horses along the route. The trail levels out again and passes several old oak trees on our left. We come to the third bridge with remains of an old dam. This is the best place to spot trout in the creek. As we cross the fourth bridge the trail breaks out into the sun. The canyon continues to widen, as meadows become more apparent. We cross two more bridges before we reach the

Oats Peak Trail junction. The trail to the left is quite steep as it climbs 1200 feet to the top of Oats Peak. We continue straight for another 0.2 mile before we reach the

Cypress Grove. Note the gnarled oaks and huge cypress trees. The shade of these beautiful trees creates a great spot for lunch or a snack. This was the site of an old cabin, since removed, built by a homesteader in the 1920's.

Retrace your steps to the Coon Creek Trailhead.

Oats Peak-Coon Creek Loop

Usage:	Hikers and Horses
Fee:	None at Present
Distance:	9.2 Miles (Loop Trip)
Elevation Gain/Loss:	1500/-1500 Feet
Approx. Hiking Time:	4 - 6 Hours
Hike Rating:	Moderately Strenuous
USGS Maps:	Morro Bay South

Best Time to Hike: All Year

Point On Route:	Distance from Starting Point Miles(Km)	Elevation
Oats Peak Trailhead	0.0 (0.0)	100
Reservoir Flats Trail Junction	0.3 (0.5)	200
Badger Trail Junction	0.6 (0.9)	375
Side trail to Valencia Peak	1.5 (2.5)	860
Oats Peak Trail Junction	2.8 (4.6)	1320
Coon Creek Trail Junction	4.3 (7.0)	320
Cypress Grove	4.5 (7.3)	320
Coon Creek Trail Junction	4.7 (7.6)	320
Rattlesnake Flats Trail Junction	6.0 (9.7)	200
Pecho Road	7.0 (11.3)	80
Bluffs Top	7.5 (12.1)	40
Corallina Cove	8.4 (13.5)	40
Bluffs Trailhead	9.2 (14.7)	120

Directions to Trailhead: From San Luis Obispo take Los Osos Valley Road to Los Osos, then continue on to the entrance of Montaña de Oro State Park via Pecho Valley Road. Drive another 2.7 miles to Park Headquarters (Visitor Center, also known as the Old Ranch House). The trailhead is located 400 feet east of the Park Headquarters on the south side of the campground.

Trail Overview: The Oats Peak-Coon Creek Loop is a combination of three other trails in the park, with a 1.1-mile trail connecting the Oats Peak and Coon Creek trails. This is a great hike that explores all aspects of Montaña de Oro State Park. It offers sweeping vistas of the California coastline, the Morros, Cuesta Ridge, and the deep valleys below. Wildflowers are abundant in spring. In summer it is best to get an early start as the trail can be hot and dry. Ticks may be present any time of the year.

Trail Description:

Oats Peak Trailhead. Our trail quickly leaves the campground area and starts a steady climb through dense vegetation of poison oak, wild raspberries, and chaparral. We climb 200 feet to the

Reservoir Flats Trail Junction. Take the right fork and continue climbing another 175 feet to the

Badger Trail Junction, which can be taken to Valencia Peak. Take the left fork here. The trail levels out for the next 0.4 mile before swinging to the right and crossing a small creek. It now climbs to a low saddle which can be brushy at times. Immediately past the saddle, the trail swings to the right again reaching a

side trail to Valencia Peak.. Take the left fork. The terrain opens up to a large grassy area and loose shale before entering a narrow gully eroded away by heavy use and winter rains. Poison oak may be hard to avoid here. Once past this gully, the trail opens up again to give great views of the ocean and Morro Bay. Oats Peak itself is still off in the distance to the east. Passing the open meadow we start a climb over a series of undulating hills traversing the ridgeline to Oats Peak. Reaching the top of the first hill, at elevation 1295', we can see a prominent Morro, Hollister Peak, with West Cuesta Ridge in the background. We continue along the ridge over the next hill before we make the final ascent to the top of

Oats Peak itself, elevation 1373. Be sure to take in all the views before continuing your journey. Leaving Oats Peak we quickly come to a

trail junction. The trail straight ahead goes to False Alan Peak, looming in the distance. This section of trail is unmaintained and possibly faint. Our journey turns right at this junction, descending along a rocky ridge into a wonderful oak woodland. After the woodland, our descent continues to wind in and out of small ravines, then down a series of switchbacks completely covered by oaks. The vegetation becomes more lush as we lose altitude. Breaking out of the oak canopy, we reach the

Coon Creek Trail Junction. Turn left here to walk a short distance to the

cypress grove. This was the site of an old cabin, long since removed. It makes for an excellent lunch break out of the hot sun. Leaving the cypress grove, we retrace our footsteps and return to the

Coon Creek Trail Junction, following Coon Creek for the rest of our journey to Pecho Road. When the trail ducks out of the dense canopy of bays, oaks, willows and many other trees, we get a peek at the ridges above. We will have the opportunity to see a variety of wildflowers including giant trillium, honeysuckle sage, false Solomon's seal, and coffeeberry. After crossing several bridges we come to the

Rattlesnake Flats Trail Junction. Horses are not allowed further on the Coon Creek trail and must turn onto the Rattlesnake Trail. Hikers may continue straight and cross a few more bridges before climbing to

Pecho Road. The parking area has a picnic table and portable restroom. Crossing Pecho Road, the Bluffs Trail is directly in front of us. It descends slightly before reaching the actual

bluffs top. Turn right here to follow the bluffs back towards the Visitor Center. Watch for Grotto Rock and many other unique rock formations that have been created by years of erosion and wave action against the cliffs below. Passing Quarry Cove we come to

Corallina Cove. This beach is accessible to the public and is a great place to see many ocean mammals, including sea otters and harbor seals basking in the sun on the rocks just offshore. The tide pools are also a good place to explore. We leave the shore for a moment to cross a wooden bridge, then turn left to follow the bluffs, traveling north once more, then turning to the east to see Spooner's Cove in the distance. Crossing one last bridge we reach the

Bluffs Trailhead, 100 yards from our starting point, Park Headquarters.

False Alan Peak

Usage:	Hikers and Horses
Fee:	None at Present
Distance:	3.7 Miles (One Way)
Elevation Gain/Loss:	+1400/-1400 Feet
Approx. Hiking Time:	4 - 6 Hours
Hike Rating:	Moderately Strenuous
USGS Maps:	Morro Bay South

Best Time to Hike: All Year

Point On Route:	Distance from Starting Point Miles(Km)	Elevation
Oats Peak Trailhead	0.0 (0.0)	100
Reservoir Flats Trail Junction	0.3 (0.5)	200
Badger Trail Junction	0.6 (0.9)	375
Valencia Cutoff Trail	1.5 (2.5)	860
Oats Peak	2.7 (4.5)	1373
Oats Peak Trail Junction	2.8 (4.6)	1320
False Alan Peak	3.7 (6.0)	1440

Directions to Trailhead: From San Luis Obispo take Los Osos Valley Road to Los Osos, then continue on to the entrance of Montaña de Oro State Park via Pecho Valley Road. Drive another 2.7 miles to Park Headquarters (Visitor Center, or Old Ranch House). The trailhead is located 400 feet east of Park Headquarters on the south side of the campground.

Trail Overview: The False Alan Peak Trail starts at the Oats Peak Trailhead. It offers a wide variety of terrain ranging from dense chaparral to open grasslands, as well as striking geological features. It also offers sweeping vistas of the California coastline, the Morros, Cuesta Ridge, and deep valleys below. Wildflowers can be abundant during the spring months. In summer it is best to get an early start as the trail can be hot and dry. Ticks may be present any time of the year. The peak acquired this name due to an incorrect label—the real Alan Peak lies across the ravine, one or two miles away.

Trail Description:

Oats Peak Trailhead. Our trail quickly leaves the campground area and starts a steady climb through dense vegetation of poison oak, wild raspberries, and chaparral. We climb 200 feet to the

Reservoir Trail Junction. We take the right fork and continue climbing another 175 feet to

Badger Trail Junction, which can be taken to Valencia Peak. Take the left fork here. The trail levels out for the next 0.4 mile before swinging to the right and crossing a small creek. It now starts a climb to a low saddle which can be overgrown with brush at times. Immediately past the saddle, the trail swings to the right again reaching a

side trail to Valencia Peak.. Take the left fork. The terrain opens up to a large grassy area and loose shale before entering a narrow gully eroded away by heavy use and winter rains. Poison oak may be hard to avoid here. Once past this gully, the trail opens up again to give great views of the ocean and Morro Bay. Oats Peak itself is still off in the distance to the east. Passing the open meadow we start a climb over a series of undulating hills traversing the ridgeline to Oats Peak. Reaching the top of the first hill, at elevation 1295', we can see a prominent Morro, Hollister Peak, with West Cuesta Ridge in the background. We continue along the ridge over the next hill before we make the final ascent to the top of

Oats Peak, elevation 1373'. Be sure to take in all the views from the top. Leaving Oats Peak, we quickly come to

Oats Peak Trail Junction. We continue straight along the ridgeline for another mile, reaching

False Alan Peak, elevation 1440', or Alan Peak Viewpoint. From here, three miles along an unmaintained trail will take us to Alan Peak, elevation 1649'. While on False Alan Peak, one can see four Morros to the north: Hollister Peak, Cerro Romauldo, Bishop Peak and Cerro San Luis.

To make a longer loop trip, return via one of the other trails, such as the Oats Peak/Coon Creek Trail.

Valencia Peak

Usage:	Hikers
Fee:	None at Present
Distance:	4.0 Miles (Round Trip)
Elevation Gain/Loss:	1200/-1200 Feet
Approx. Hiking Time:	2-4 Hours
Hike Rating:	Moderate
USGS Maps:	Morro Bay South

Best Time to Hike: All Year

Point On Route:	Distance from Starting Point Miles(Km)	Elevation
Valencia Peak Trailhead	0.0 (0.0)	120
Rattlesnake Trail Junction	0.1 (0.2)	140
Badger Trail Junction	0.8 (1.3)	500
Oats Peak Cutoff Trail	1.6 (2.5)	1047
Valencia Peak	1.9 (3.0)	1347
Oats Peak Cutoff Trail	2.2 (3.5)	1047
Oats Peak Trail	2.5 (4.0)	820
Badger Trail Junction	3.4 (5.6)	375
Reservoir Flats Trail Junction	3.7 (6.0)	200
Oats Peak Trailhead	4.0 (6.5)	100

Directions to Trailhead: From San Luis Obispo, take Los Osos Valley Road to Los Osos and continue to the entrance of Montaña de Oro State Park via Pecho Valley Road. Drive another 2.7 miles to the Park Headquarters (Visitor Center, or Old Ranch House). The trailhead is located 500 feet south on the east side of Pecho Valley Road across from the Montaña de Oro Bluff Trailhead

Trail Overview: On a clear day, Valencia Peak, elevation 1347', offers spectacular views from Point Sal to the south to Piedras Blancas to the north. Fog is frequent, especially in summer. The trail starts inland with a gradual ascent through fields of colorful wildflowers which in the spring include poppies, paintbrush, goldfields, milkmaids, lupine, mustard, morning glory and violets. On your way to the summit you may hear an occasional rattlesnake, and once on top, look for soaring birds, including hawks and turkey vultures. The return trip takes you to the Oats Peak Cutoff trail, then returns via the Oats Peak Trail.

Trail Description:

Valencia Peak Trailhead. Our trail starts east with a gradual ascent through an open field where we quickly come to the

Rattlesnake Flats Trail Junction, aptly named for the many snakes that have been found in the area. Continuing straight through the field we come to the base of a small hill. The trail swings to the right over a small knoll, then descends slightly before turning left into an eroded ravine, part of an old jeep trail. Climbing, the trail then crosses an open shale slope into another open field gradually ascending to

Badger Trail Junction. The trail to the right goes to Badger Flat and is a possible return route. The trail to the left descends steeply to the Oats Peak Trail. We will continue straight, and climb several steep switchbacks to the next knoll. Please pay close attention to the trail and avoid the many shortcuts that cause erosion. Once on top, stop to take in the views of the surrounding hills and coastline. In spring, this knoll is covered with a host of wildflowers. With the trail now level for 0.1 mile we can take in the beauty of the park itself. Having crossed the knoll, the trail gets very steep. Take your time and watch your footing on this slippery shale slope. Please use the many short switchbacks. We finally reach the

Oats Peak Cutoff Trail at elevation 1047'. Take a short rest here before making the final ascent of Valencia Peak. Take the trail to the right over three more switchbacks across shale slopes. These rocks can be quite slippery and roll out from underfoot. Reaching the top of

Valencia Peak, we find a survey marker designating the peak. On top you can see Hollister Peak, Morro Rock, Coon Creek, and the bluff below. This makes a great lunch stop. Leaving Valencia Peak we descend to the

Oats Peak Cutoff. Continue straight, not left, to traverse the north side of Valencia Peak. The trail then takes a quick right-hand turn, then starts a steady descent through blackberry bushes and other dense vegetation before reaching the

Oats Peak Trail. For a more challenging trip, continue right to Oats Peak, then return via Coon Creek. Our route turns left here across an open meadow and swings left before we descend to a small seasonal stream over numerous railroad tie steps. After crossing the stream the trail is level for the next 0.4 mile, eventually reaching the Badger Trail junction. The left trail climbs steeply to the Valencia Peak Trail. We continue down to the right for 0.3 mile, descending 175 feet to the

Reservoir Flats Trail Junction. Keeping left we can see the park headquarters, our final destination. We traverse above the campground before reaching the

Oats Peak Trailhead. Once back on the road, it is a short distance back to your car by Park Headquarters.

SPOONER'S COVE

Reservoir Flats

Usage:	Hikers Only
Fee:	None at Present
Distance:	2.0 Miles (Round Trip)
Elevation Gain/Loss:	+200/-200 Feet
Approx. Hiking Time:	1 - 2 Hours
Hike Rating:	Easy
USGS Maps:	Morro Bay South

Best Time to Hike: All Year

Point On Route:	Distance from Starting Point Miles(Km)	Elevation
Oats Peak Trailhead	0.0 (0.0)	100
Reservoir Flats Trail Junction	0.3 (0.5)	200
Reservoir Flats	0.4 (0.6)	250
Islay Creek Cutoff	1.5 (2.4)	120
Montaña de Oro Campground	1.7 (2.7)	100
Oats Peak Trailhead	2.0 (3.2)	100

Directions to Trailhead: From San Luis Obispo, take Los Osos Valley Road to Los Osos, then continue on Los Osos Valley Road to the entrance of Montaña de Oro State Park via Pecho Valley Road. Drive another 2.7 miles to the Park Headquarters (Visitor Center, or Old Ranch House). The trailhead is located 400 feet east of Park Headquarters on the south side of the campground, called the Enroute area.

Trail Overview: Reservoir Flats is an easy trail on the Islay Creek drainage. As we traverse the low-lying coastal sage scrub regions of the Park, we encounter ferns, pines, and thick vegetation. This trail offers good views of the coastline from its higher elevations and then a delightful stroll through the Montaña de Oro campground upon its return to the Oats Peak Trailhead, as well as wildflowers in the spring. A short side trip to Islay Creek itself and a visit to the crumbling dam on Islay Creek are additional options.

Trail Description:

Oats Peak Trailhead. Our trail quickly leaves the Enroute campground area and starts a steady climb through dense vegetation of poison oak, blackberries and sage scrub. We climb 200 feet to the

Reservoir Flats Trail Junction. The Oats Peak Trail continues to the right. We turn left here and climb gently to Reservoir Flats. This man-made reservoir is fed by a dozen springs. It is less than one acre in size and a few feet deep, and dries out in summer and fall. The Spooner family farmed the area in the early 1900s. A waterwheel churn produced butter and cream to be shipped to San Francisco. Continuing around the reservoir, we climb to an elevation of 300 feet. The campground lies below us, with Spooner's Cove in the distance. From here we start a gradual descent to reach the

Islay Creek Trail Cutoff. A right turn here takes the hiker to Islay Road. To reach a hidden trail to an old dam, turn right on Islay Road. Our trail continues straight along Islay Creek itself. The lush vegetation along the creek includes willows, cottonwoods, many ferns, blackberry vines, stinging nettle and poison oak. You may see a dusky-footed woodrat nest along the trail. The trail then rises slightly above the creek, offering better views of the canyon just before reaching the

Montaña de Oro Campground. From here follow the paved road 0.3 mile through the campground to the

Oats Peak Trailhead. Take time to enjoy the stillness of the area and the beauty of the pine trees.

M. Foster
SPOONER'S COVE

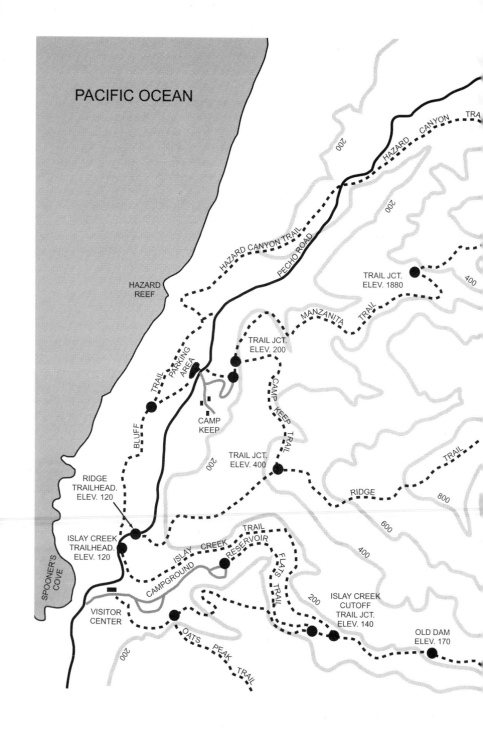

Montaña de Oro North

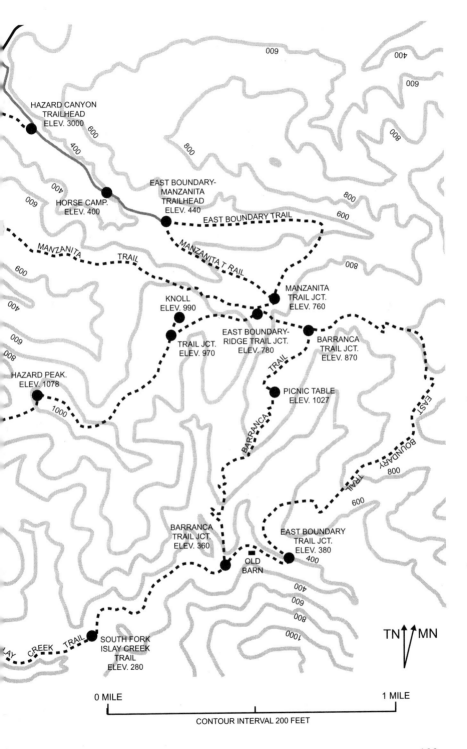

HAZARD CANYON
TRAILHEAD
ELEV. 3000

HORSE CAMP.
ELEV. 400

EAST BOUNDARY-
MANZANITA
TRAILHEAD
ELEV. 440

EAST BOUNDARY TRAIL

MANZANITA TRAIL

MANZANITA TRAIL

MANZANITA
TRAIL JCT.
ELEV. 760

KNOLL
ELEV. 990

EAST BOUNDARY-
RIDGE TRAIL JCT.
ELEV. 780

BARRANCA
TRAIL JCT.
ELEV. 870

TRAIL JCT.
ELEV. 970

HAZARD PEAK.
ELEV. 1078

TRAIL

BARRANCA

PICNIC TABLE
ELEV. 1027

EAST

BOUNDARY

TRAIL

BARRANCA
TRAIL JCT.
ELEV. 360

OLD
BARN

EAST BOUNDARY
TRAIL JCT.
ELEV. 380

CREEK TRAIL

SOUTH FORK
ISLAY CREEK
TRAIL
ELEV. 280

TN MN

0 MILE

1 MILE

CONTOUR INTERVAL 200 FEET

109

Islay Creek

Usage:	Hikers, Horses and Mountain Bikes
Fee:	None at Present
Distance:	3.0 Miles (One Way)
Elevation Gain/Loss:	+400/-100 Feet
Approx. Hiking Time:	2 - 4 Hours
Hike Rating:	Moderate
USGS Maps:	Morro Bay South

Best Time to Hike: All Year

Point On Route:	Distance from Starting Point Miles(Km)	Elevation
Islay Creek Trailhead	0.0 (0.0)	100
Reservoir Flats Trail Cutoff	1.0 (1.6)	140
Old Dam Trail	1.3 (2.1)	170
South Fork Islay Trail	2.0 (3.2)	280
Barranca Trail.	2.7 (4.3)	360
East Boundary Trail	3.0 (4.8)	380

Directions to Trailhead: From San Luis Obispo, take Los Osos Valley Road to Los Osos, then continue on Los Osos Valley Road to the entrance of Montaña de Oro State Park via Pecho Valley Road. Drive another 2.3 miles to a signed trailhead on the left. Park on the grass across from the trailhead. Park Headquarters (Visitor Center, or Old Ranch House) is 0.3 mile further along the road. The trail is just around the bend behind a locked gate.

Trail Overview: The Islay Creek Trail is a well-maintained old ranch road that traverses the center of Montaña de Oro State Park. It offers a glimpse of history with a dam and old barn. These date back to the days when Montaña de Oro was part of the Pecho Ranch. Being a ranch road, one can enjoy the sights without concern over poison oak or poor footing. It is also a good place to practice riding a mountain bike. It can be combined with either the Barranca or East Boundary Trail to make a delightful loop hike.

Trail Description:

Islay Creek Trailhead. This trail, really a wide road, begins by following Islay Creek, 50 feet below to the right. The campground can be seen across the creek. Cuts made into the hillside to build the road show the geology of the area by exposing shale formations. Valencia Peak can be seen high to the right. The canyon itself is quite lush with thick chaparral to our left and bush poppies along the road. At the one-mile point we come to the

Reservoir Flats Cutoff Trail. Continuing along the road, we come to another, possibly faint, trail junction leading to the

Old Dam. It continues to be eroded by floods. The dam itself is not easy to reach, but it can be seen from the road. Water power was used for generating electricity and churning butter during the early 1900s when Montaña de Oro was part of the Pecho Ranch. This spot is also a great place for cooling off on a warm day. The road continues to wind uphill. The canyon widens as Islay Creek splits into two creeks and reaches the

South Fork Islay Trail. This trail was a favorite of Ed West, a former Sierra Club hike leader. The road climbs ever so gently up the canyon. We cross a bridge or two before coming to the

Barranca Trail on our left. We continue straight across a bridge with an old abandoned barn on our right. Feel free to explore the barn, but watch out for snakes that may have slithered in looking for shade. Two-tenths of a mile past the barn we come the

East Boundary Trail, and a bit further a locked gate. Please do not go beyond the gate, because it marks private property.

Ridge Trail-Barranca Loop

Usage:	Hikers, Horses and Mountain Bikers
Fee:	None at Present
Distance:	2.0 Miles (Round Trip)
Elevation Gain/Loss:	+1500/-1500 Feet
Approx. Hiking Time:	3 - 5 Hours
Hike Rating:	Moderate
USGS Maps:	Morro Bay South

Best Time to Hike: All Year

Point On Route:	Distance from Starting Point Miles(Km)	Elevation
Ridge Trailhead	0.0 (0.0)	120
Camp Keep Trail Junction	0.6 (0.9)	400
Hazard Peak	1.9 (0.6)	1076
Trail Junction	2.5 (4.0)	970
East Boundary Trail Junction	2.9 (4.5)	780
Barranca Trail Junction	3.3 (5.3)	870
Islay Creek Road	4.3 (6.9)	360
South Fork Islay Creek Trail	5.0 (8.0)	280
Old Dam	5.7 (9.1)	170
Reservoir Flats Trail Cutoff	6.0 (9.6)	140
Islay Creek Trailhead	7.0 (11.2)	100

Directions to Trailhead: From San Luis Obispo, take Los Osos Valley Road to Los Osos, then continue to the entrance of Montaña de Oro State Park via Pecho Valley Road. Drive another 2.3 miles to a signed trailhead on the left. Park on the grassy area across from the trailhead. Park Headquarters (Visitor Center, or Old Ranch House) is 0.3 mile further along the road.

Trail Overview: The Ridge Trail Loop explores the northern side of Montaña de Oro State Park and is used by hikers, mountain bikers and horses. Please observe the standard right-of-way rules on these trails (see the section Hiking in SLO County for rules). The trail itself wanders through thick chaparral, then ascends to open grassland dotted with wildflowers in late winter, spring and early summer months. On Hazard Peak there is a bench where you can enjoy 360-degree views of Morro Bay, Montaña de Oro, the Morros, and West Cuesta Ridge.

Trail Description:

Ridge Trailhead. We begin on a sometimes sandy and dusty trail with chaparral on both sides. After it swings to the left, we climb to an open mesa with a eucalyptus grove. Hazard Peak can be seen in the distance. Climbing, we cross the mesa coming to the unmarked

Camp Keep Trail Junction. This trail was put in by volunteers in mid-2000 as an alternate route to Camp Keep. Our trail continues straight, then turns right (south) to round the base of a steep hill, giving us a glimpse into the Islay Creek Drainage, Valencia Peak, and the Bluff Trail. Soon the trail starts the climb of this 600-foot hill. The vegetation turns to open grass along a ridge. Wildflowers thrive here. We continue our ascent along the ridge, hiking over loose shale. The trail comes to a fence, then makes a sharp turn to the right before the final ascent to the top of

Hazard Peak, elevation 1076 feet. At Hazard Peak there is a bench for resting, and tools for trail maintenance. Please leave these tools with the bench. Hazard Peak offers 360-degree views of Montaña de Oro Sate Park and the ridges beyond. Hollister Peak, Cerro Alto, Morro Rock and Black Hill can all be seen from this vantage point. Leaving Hazard Peak, the trail is quite rocky as it traverses the ridge top. Once on the other end of the ridge, the trail forks. Going straight will take you to the knoll in front of you. Take the right fork down the rocky slope into thick brush. A few hundred yards ahead we come to the

East Boundary Trail junction. The left forks take you to the Manzanita Trail and to the horse camp. The right fork, our path, takes us to the eastern part of the park. We start a climb to the saddle ahead to reach the

Barranca Trail Junction. Straight ahead is the continuation of the East Boundary Trail. It ends up on Islay Creek Road. We turn right to climb to the top of a knoll, elevation 1022 feet—just past the knoll is a side trail to a picnic bench for a nice lunch stop. Leaving the picnic bench, we start our 500-foot descent down the ridge to

Islay Creek Road. An abandoned barn lies just up the road on our left. We turn right to follow Islay Creek Road west to Pecho Road. The road is quite wide, making it a leisurely hike compared to the rugged trails we have left behind. Take in the views of the canyon along the way. 0.9 mile from Barranca Trail, we reach the

South Fork Islay Trail. This is a loop trail to explore the hill across the stream. Our path stays on the road for another mile, reaching the

Old Dam, used for power generation and a butter churn when Montaña de Oro was part of Pecho Ranch. The dam is not always easy to reach, but can make a nice place to cool off on a warm day. Just past the dam is the

Reservoir Flats Trail Cutoff. This trail takes you across Islay Creek and directly to the campground and visitor center. We continue straight along Islay Creek Road for another mile, to reach the end of our journey at

Islay Creek Trailhead.

CHUMASH SHELL MOUND
IN THE DUNES, MORRO BAY SAND SPIT

Morro Bay Sandspit

Usage:	Hikers, Horses, Partly Wheelchair Accessible
Fee:	None at Present
Distance:	5.3 Miles (One Way to Tip of Sandspit)
Elevation Gain/Loss:	-100 Feet
Approx. Hiking Time:	3 - 5 Hours
Hike Rating:	Moderate
USGS Maps:	Morro Bay South

Best Time to Hike: All Year

Directions to Trailhead: From San Luis Obispo, take Los Osos Valley Road to Los Osos and continue to the entrance of Montaña de Oro State Park via Pecho Valley Road. Drive another 0.8 mile to Sandspit Road (AT&T Road). Turn right and drive 0.5 mile to the parking area.

Trail Overview: The Morro Bay Sandspit is a 3.5-mile point of land that forms the western boundary of Morro Bay Estuary. There are other ways to access Morro Bay Sandspit, but this is the easiest. The Sandspit has much to offer the explorer: crashing waves, dune wildflowers, views of the Morros, and a small band of deer that roam this fragile habitat. The Chumash have left traces of their life here, most noticeably middens (piles of seashells). Be sure to bring at least a windbreaker on this trip—weather can change dramatically in a short period of time.

Trail Description:

Sandspit Trailhead. The trail leaves the western edge of the parking lot along a boardwalk that extends 0.2 mile and drops 100 feet to the Pacific Ocean. Partway down the boardwalk we find a viewing platform, wheelchair accessible. Once on the beach, we can head north towards Morro Rock, five miles away. The pounding surf can be a hiker's delight, but on windy days the traveler is pelted with sand and ocean mist. A series of numbered posts have been installed, approximately 0.5 mile apart. This beach was used for training during World War II. The large telephone posts lying sideways were intended to look like cannons guarding the shore. If you make it to the end

115

of the Sandspit there are two breakwaters, built to protect the entrance to the bay.

On your return trip, take a more inland route for great views of Morro Bay, Black Hill, Los Osos and Baywood. A unique flora and fauna is found in some of the inland valleys. You might even see a small herd of dear grazing.

Note: Walking on soft sand takes more energy than appears at first sight. For a harder walking surface, head west towards the beach.

San Luis Obispo

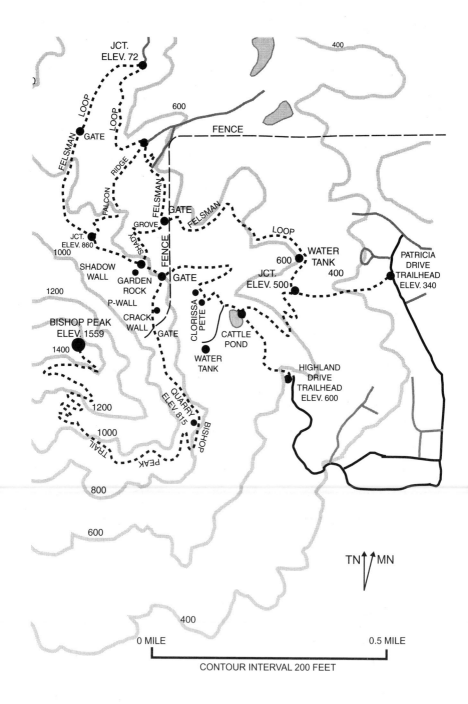

Bishop Peak/Felsman Loop

Bishop Peak

Usage: Hikers, Climbers and Dogs on Leash
Fee: None
Distance: 2.2 Miles (One Way)
Elevation Gain/Loss: +1200 Feet
Approx. Hiking Time: 3 - 4 Hours
Hike Rating: Moderate
USGS Maps: San Luis Obispo

Best Time to Hike: All Year, Mornings and Evenings in Summer

Point On Route:	Distance from Starting Point Miles(Km)	Elevation
Patricia Drive Trailhead	0.0 (0.0)	340
Bishop Peak Trail Sign	0.2 (0.3)	500
Cattle Pond	0.5 (0.8)	660
Bishop Peak/Felsman Loop Junction	0.8 (1.3)	840
Quarry	1.1 (1.7)	820
Old Foothill Trail	1.4 (2.3)	960
Saddle of Bishop Peak Summit	2.2 (3.5)	1500

Directions to Trailhead: From San Luis Obispo take Santa Rosa Street, Highway 1, to Foothill Blvd. Turn left on Foothill toward Los Osos Valley Road. Turn right onto Patricia Drive and follow it past the Highland Drive stop sign, to the 800 block of Patricia Drive, ¼ mile. There is a large open area on your left. Look for a "TRAIL" sign on the left, and four black posts. This is the Bishop Peak Trailhead. If you reach Twinridge Drive, you have gone too far. Park on the Bishop Peak side of Patricia Drive if possible.

Trail Overview: Bishop Peak, at 1559 feet, is tallest of the Nine Sisters, a volcanic range that extends from Morro Bay to San Luis Obispo. It was named by the Mission padres, who thought that the three spires on top resembled a bishop's miter cap.

The Sierra Club and California Conservation Corps (CCC) constructed the Bishop Trail in 1998/9. The trail is a culmination of many years of effort by the Sierra Club and other organizations and agencies. The Bunnell, Gnesa,

Ferrini, and Madonna families donated or sold land to make the Bishop Peak Natural Reserve a reality. This is a wonderful trail with unparalleled views along the Morros Range, encompassing diverse habitats of grasslands, oak woodlands and dense chaparral. Its proximity to San Luis Obispo makes it one of the most popular trails in the county.

If you wish to do a longer version of this hike, you might want to take the Felsman Loop first, then climb Bishop Peak itself from where the Felsman Loop rejoins the Bishop Peak Trail.

As part of the negotiations to create the Bishop Peak Natural Reserve, and due to the high usage of the area, only hikers and climbers are allowed access to the area. Please respect this wish by not bringing your bicycle into the Bishop Peak Natural Reserve.

Trail Description:

Patricia Drive Trailhead: The trail starts along a dirt utility access road with a pedestrian gate. Bishop Peak is already visible from here. Open hills and oaks beckon the hiker to the top. The trail then climbs 150 feet to the

Bishop Peak Trail Sign. The Bishop Peak Trail goes left up the hill. For a longer hike, continue up the road along the Felsman Loop to the water tank. The trail eventually rejoins the Bishop Peak Trail. Our route continues its steady climb up four switchbacks. A few large rocks make a good rest stop to enjoy the views. Along this stretch of the trail, you may see shooting stars, yellow violets and a mariposa lily or two. Passing under several oaks, the trail reaches the

Cattle Pond. Turn right and continue along another utility road for 100 feet. Take the trail directly ahead as we continue up the hill toward the fence line. The trail passes by the Clorissa and Pete Boulders, then takes a gentle climb to a low ridge. Here we get our first views of Chorro Valley and West Cuesta Ridge. Cerro Alto can be seen in the distance. Following the ridge, we pass through a pedestrian gate and reach the

Bishop Peak/Felsman Loop Junction. Rejoining the Bishop Peak Trail, take the left fork across an open field, then into an oak-covered forest. The trail is rocky from this point on. In a short distance the trail comes to a fork by Crack-Wall, heavily used by climbers. The left fork, our trail, passes through a pedestrian gate, then traverses a shady oak woodland before reaching the

Quarry high above Bishop Peak Elementary School and the City of San Luis Obispo. We now drop off the quarry for a quick 30-foot descent, then start a climb up three switchbacks. With some stretch of imagination, you may see a grumpy face on "Sour Puss Rock." Once past the switchbacks, the trail climbs a bit more before leveling out and offering views of Foothill Blvd., Cerro San Luis and Laguna Lake. Continuing, we come to the

Old Foothill Boulevard Trail. The Madonna family owns the lower portions of the land, and technically you are trespassing if you access Bishop Peak up this trail.

We continue around the peak. From here the trail again starts its ascent of Bishop Peak. Finally, we reach a series of eight switchbacks that complete our climb of this magnificent peak. In clear weather, our climb offers an ever-expanding view south along the coastline to Mussel Rock and Oceano Dunes. Take your time up this steep trail. We now reach the

Saddle of the Summit of Bishop Peak, between two of the three corners of the bishop's miter. From here on, the trails are not maintained. The rock to the right is the easiest to climb. Please be careful! The north-facing slopes are steep, unstable and full of poison oak .

BISHOP PEAK

Felsman Loop

Usage:	Hikers, Climbers, Horses and Dogs on Leash
Fee:	None
Distance:	2.7 Miles (Round Trip)
Elevation Gain/Loss:	+700/-700 Feet
Approx. Hiking Time:	1-3 Hours
Hike Rating:	Easy to Moderate
USGS Maps:	San Luis Obispo

Best Time to Hike: All Year

Point On Route:	Distance from Starting Point Miles(Km)	Elevation
Patricia Drive Trailhead	0.0 (0.0)	340
Bishop Peak Trail Sign	0.2 (0.3)	500
Water Tank	0.3 (0.5)	600
Pedestrian Gate/Shady Grove Junction	0.7 (1.1)	680
Falcon Ridge Junction	0.9 (1.4)	680
Ranch Road Junction	1.2 (1.9)	720
Falcon Ridge Junction	1.7 (2.7)	860
Garden Rock/Shady Grove Junction	1.8 (2.9)	840
Bishop Peak/Felsman Loop Junction	1.9 (3.0)	840
Cattle Pond	2.2 (3.5)	660
Bishop/Felsman Loop Junction	2.4 (3.8)	500
Patricia Drive Trailhead	2.7 (4.3)	340

Directions to Trailhead: From San Luis Obispo take Santa Rosa Street north to Foothill Blvd. Turn left on Foothill toward Los Osos Valley Road. Turn right onto Patricia Drive and follow it past the Highland Drive stop sign, to the 800 block of Patricia Drive, ¼ mile. There is a large open area on your left. Look for a "TRAIL" sign and four black posts on the left. This is the Bishop Peak Trailhead. If you reach Twinridge Drive, you have gone too far. Park on the Bishop Peak side of Patricia Drive if possible.

Trail Overview: Bishop Peak, at 1559 feet, is the tallest of the Nine Sisters, a volcanic range that extends from Morro Bay to San Luis Obispo. Bishop

Peak was named by the padres of Mission San Luis Obispo, who felt that the three spires on top resembled a bishop's miter cap.

The Sierra Club constructed the Felsman Loop, named after Gary Felsman who made this acquisition a success and coordinated the construction of the Felsman Loop and Bishop Trail in 1998/9. The trail is a culmination of many years of effort by the Sierra Club and other organizations and agencies. A special word of thanks is due the Bunnell, Gnesa, Ferrini and Madonna families, who sold or donated land to make the Bishop Peak Natural Reserve a reality. The Felsman Loop allows us to explore grassland, oak woodlands, and chaparral ecosystems. This trail also rewards the hiker with views of Chumash Peak and Chorro Valley.

As part of the negotiations to create the Bishop Peak Natural Reserve, and due to the high usage of the area, wheeled transportation is not allowed access to the area. Please respect this wish by exploring Bishop Peak Natural Reserve on foot, no matter how tempting it might be to ride a mountain bike. The trail is well marked and maintained.

Trail Description:

Patricia Drive Trailhead: The trail starts along a dirt utility access road with a pedestrian gate. Bishop Peak towers above the trailhead, and open hills and oaks beckon the hiker. The trail then climbs 150 feet to the

Bishop Peak Trail Sign. The Bishop Peak Trail goes left up the hill. Our trail continues straight up the paved road to the

water tank. Skirt the fence on the right side of the water tank, where the Felsman Loop begins. The trail now swings left into an oak woodland, crosses a seasonal creek, and climbs to a knoll for a view of Bunnell Ranch. From the knoll, the trail descends across an open meadow, possibly boggy in winter. It then enters the forest again, crossing a small stream before reaching the

pedestrian gate. This is the junction with the Shady Grove Trail, which goes left. The Felsman Loop turns right to follow an old ranch road a short distance downhill. When the road makes a sharp right turn, follow our trail straight up the hill. After two short switchbacks, the trail crosses another old road before reaching the

Falcon Ridge Trail Junction The Felsman Loop continues across the road, entering another oak forest as it descends to a bridge over a small stream. Here the terrain changes into chaparral. West Cuesta Ridge spreads out to the east. Watch for the many spring flowers and the occasional pack rat nest along the trail. The trail reaches the farthest of the three

ranch roads on the Bishop Peak Reserve. Turn left and follow the ridge line. Be sure to take your time and enjoy the views of the valley, as well as the different perspective of Chumash and Bishop Peaks. The trail passes through a gate, then makes a short climb to reach the

Falcon Ridge Trail. Taking the right fork, continue along the road. Ignore the old cow path and continue left along the road. Watch for the

Garden Rock on the right, shaded by a huge oak tree. Ignore the junction with the Shady Grove Trail and continue straight along the road, then take the left fork to reach the

Bishop Peak/Felsman Loop Junction For a longer hike, turn right to ascend the summit of Bishop Peak itself at 1559 feet. The Felsman Loop passes through the pedestrian gate, follows the ridge, and switches back as we descend to the Clorissa and Pete boulders before reaching the maintenance road. Follow this road and turn left when you reach the

Patricia Avenue Trail sign. The trail continues down four switchbacks and rejoins the maintenance road. This is marked by the

Bishop Peak Trail Sign. Turn right and follow the road back to the

Patricia Drive Trailhead.

LAGUNA LAKE

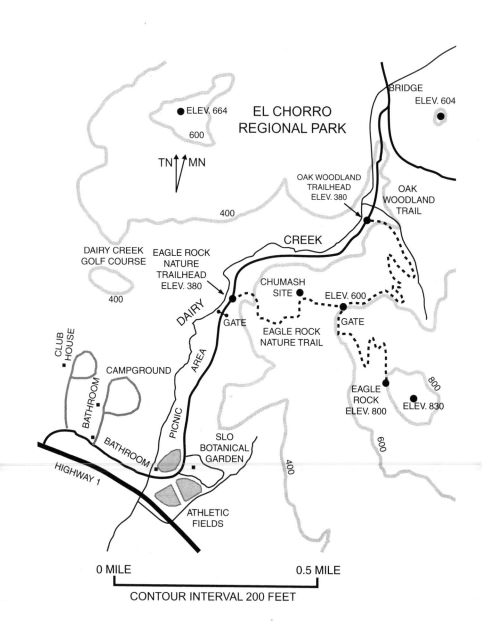

Eagle Rock

Eagle Rock Nature Trail

Usage:	Hikers and Dogs on Leash
Fee:	Weekend Fee if Applicable
Distance:	2.2 Miles (Round Trip)
Elevation Gain/Loss:	+720/-720 Feet
Approx. Hiking Time:	2-3 Hours Round Trip
Hike Rating:	Easy
USGS Maps:	San Luis Obispo

Best Time to Hike: All Year

Point On Route:	Distance from Starting Point Miles(Km)	Elevation
Eagle Rock Nature Trailhead	0.0 (0.0)	320
Chumash Mortars	0.2 (0.3)	560
Oak Woodland Trail	0.4 (0.5)	560
Eagle Rock	0.7 (1.1)	800
Oak Woodland Trail	1.0 (1.6)	560
Open Meadow	1.5 (2.4)	560
Paved Road	1.8 (3.0)	360

Directions to Trailhead: The trailhead is found across from Cuesta College at El Chorro Regional Park. From San Luis Obispo, take Highway 1 North towards Cuesta College and turn east (right) at the first of two turn signals to El Chorro Regional Park. Follow the signs to the Day Use area, passing the ball fields and Botanical Garden. Park in the Day Use area at the end of the park, just before the locked gate.

Trail Overview: The 1.8-mile Eagle Rock Self-Guided Nature Trail explores a section of El Chorro Regional Park. The trail was constructed by the County Parks Service in 1992 and made into a nature trail by the Santa Lucia Chapter of the Sierra Club in 1995. This easy trail is great for beginner hikers and offers many examples of coastal flora and fauna. Late winter to early summer wildflowers include shooting stars, blue eyed grass, hummingbird sage, checker bloom and red maids. The trail offers many views of the Morros, a chain of ancient volcanoes formed 25 million years ago that are part of the Franciscan Formation. East of El Chorro Regional Park is Cuesta Ridge, part of the Los Padres National Forest. The Highway 41 fire in 1994 devastated this area, but signs of new growth point to a full recovery within 20 years. Be sure to take a brochure to get more information about flora and fauna along the trail.

Trail Description:

Eagle Rock Nature Trailhead: Walk through the pedestrian gate along the road 0.1 mile to the actual start of the trail. From here we start a slow and steady climb through a well-established oak grove. Notice the variety of trees as well as black sage, monkey flowers, and lichen on the rocks. A trail sign points left. Follow this trail a short distance to a vantage point of El Chorro Regional Park and to a point of interest,

Chumash mortar holes, Trail Post #3. These holes were made by Chumash Indians for grinding acorns. The trail is level for another 0.1 mile, reaching the junction of

Oak Woodland Trail and the trail to Eagle Rock. We will turn right and pass through a pedestrian gate, then turn left to ascend the hill via a few switchbacks before leveling off for the final 0.1 mile, reaching

Eagle Rock itself. At an elevation of 760 feet, this point offers views of Camp San Luis Obispo and the botanical area below. Visible in the distance is the chain of ancient volcanoes known as the Morros. On a clear day you can see Morro Rock next to the PG&E (Duke) power plant, and, to the east, West Cuesta Ridge, along with a good portion of Camp San Luis Obispo. Retracing our steps 0.3 mile we return to the

trail junction. We continue straight and enter an oak forest. The trail swings right before reaching Nature Post #9. The wood piles above and below the trail are made by wood rats. The trail is now level and soon reaches a switchback turning sharply to the left. Passing snowberrries at post #10, the trail continues to traverse the hill. After two more switchbacks and a growth of hummingbird sage, we reach an

open meadow high above El Chorro Regional Park. Leaving the meadow, the trail turns to the right, then descends to a year-round stream covered with lush ferns. Following the stream we come to post #15, a favorite of botanist Dr. Shirley Sparlings due to the abundance of lichen on the large rocks. Immediately past the rocks we return to the

paved road. Turn left here to return to the trailhead, 0.4 mile. Be sure to stop at post #16 to view the sycamore trees. One of these is patronized by acorn woodpeckers, which have stored hundreds of acorns in its trunk.

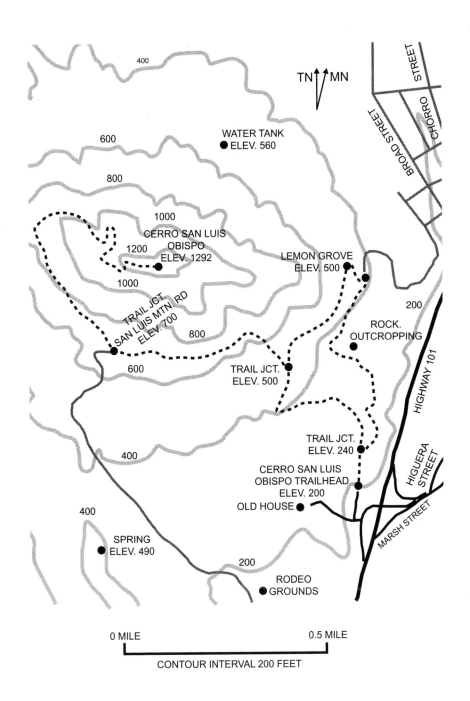

Maino Open Space

Maino Open Space
(Cerro San Luis Obispo)

Usage:	Hikers, Mountain Bikers and Dogs on Leash
Fee:	None
Distance:	2.2 Mile Loop
Elevation Gain/Loss:	+400/-400 Feet
Approx. Hiking Time:	1-2 Hours Round Trip
Hike Rating:	Easy to Moderate
USGS Maps:	San Luis Obispo

Best Time to Hike: All Year

Point On Route:	Distance from Starting Point Miles(Km)	Elevation
Maino Open Space Trailhead	0.0 (0.0)	200
Boundary Sign	1.1 (1.8)	420
Lemon Grove	1.3 (2.1)	500
San Luis Mountain Trail Junction	1.7 (2.7)	500
Maino Open Space Trailhead	2.2 (3.5)	200

Directions to Trailhead: The Maino Open Space Trailhead is located off the Marsh Street onramp of southbound Highway 101. From downtown San Luis Obispo take Higuera Street to the intersection with Marsh Street and proceed as if to take 101 South. Immediately after the freeway underpass you will see a road on the right hand side. Turn here and right again into the parking area.

Trail Overview: Cerro San Luis Obispo, or San Luis Mountain, offers two different areas to explore. We will only describe the trail to the lemon grove, which is on public land. The very popular upper trail to the top of San Luis Mountain is on private land owned by the Madonna family. Hiking on this property is done at one's own risk and is subject to any restrictions that may be in place at the time. The Lemon Grove trail described here skirts the east side of San Luis Mountain and is a far gentler hike than the climb to the top. It makes a pleasant family hike. Depending on which trail you select, you will be treated to splendid views of the surrounding area. This may include views of San Luis Obispo, Bishop Peak, Morro Bay to the north, and Pismo and Avila Beach to the south.

San Luis Mountain, at 1292 feet, is one of the Morros or Nine Sisters of San Luis Obispo County. It is sometimes called Madonna Mountain, although the "M" on the mountain stands for Mission High School, not Madonna as it is often believed.

Trail Description:

Maino Open Space Trailhead: Pass through the pedestrian gate at the end of the parking lot and follow this old ranch road up the hill. In approximately 500 feet, look for the Lemon Grove trail sign on the right. It contours the east-facing slope of San Luis Mountain in many short ups and downs. Stop to enjoy the city views and the occasional freight train winding its way up or down Cuesta Grade. This trail can be messy in wet weather. In approximately one mile we reach a eucalyptus grove and the

Open Space Boundary Sign. Please respect this sign and follow the trail as it makes a sharp left turn, continuing along a more level grassy area. The city now lies to our left. In approximately .2 mile we pass a squeaky metal gate and enter a grove of eucalyptus and Monterey pines. To our right is the

Lemon Grove after which this trail was named. Continuing, the trail passes through an area of cactus mixed with poison oak, then traverses a small but delightful grove of shady oaks over a seasonal spring, ascending steeply to rejoin the

San Luis Mountain Trail Junction. Turn left here to return to the parking lot. The trail up San Luis Mountain goes right. It involves an 800-foot climb across private property. If you should choose to take this trail, be sure to respect the rights of the property owner by not spooking cattle, closing all gates, leaving intact any fences along this route, and otherwise doing what the owner requests. Our route goes left on the main road, descending through cactus groves on both sides of the trail and passing the trail entry point. We descend on this broad road to return to the

Maino Open Space Trailhead.

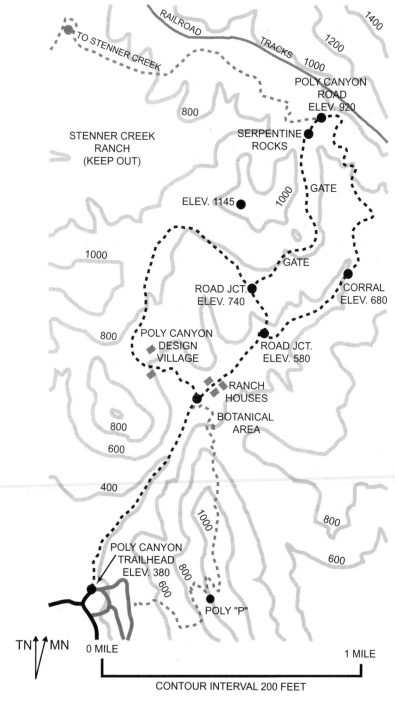

RAILROAD

TRACKS

TO STENNER CREEK

POLY CANYON ROAD ELEV. 920

1400

1200

1000

800

STENNER CREEK RANCH (KEEP OUT)

SERPENTINE ROCKS

ELEV. 1145

1000

GATE

GATE

1000

ROAD JCT. ELEV. 740

CORRAL ELEV. 680

POLY CANYON DESIGN VILLAGE

800

ROAD JCT. ELEV. 580

RANCH HOUSES

BOTANICAL AREA

800

600

400

1000

800

600

POLY CANYON TRAILHEAD ELEV. 380

800

600

POLY "P"

TN   MN

0 MILE   1 MILE

CONTOUR INTERVAL 200 FEET

Poly Canyon

Poly Canyon Loop

Usage:	Hikers, Horses, Mountain Bikers and Dogs
Fee:	Campus Parking Fee if Applicable
Distance:	4.7 Miles (Round Trip)
Elevation Gain/Loss:	+560/-560 Feet
Approx. Hiking Time:	2-3 Hours Round Trip
Hike Rating:	Moderate
USGS Maps:	San Luis Obispo

Best Time to Hike: All Year

Point On Route:	Distance from Starting Point Miles(Km)	Elevation
Poly Canyon Trailhead	0.0 (0.0)	380
Road to Right	0.4 (0.6)	440
Wooden Bridge .	0.7 (1.1)	480
Ranch House	0.8 (1.3)	500
Road Junction	1.2 (1.9)	580
Road Junction	1.4 (2.2)	740
Gate	1.6 (2.6)	800
Wire Gate	1.8 (3.0)	800
Serpentine Rocks	2.2 (3.4)	920
Poly Canyon Road	2.3 (3.6)	920
Gate and Corral	3.2 (5.1)	680
Road Junction	3.5 (5.6)	480
Poly Canyon Trailhead	4.7 (7.6)	380

Directions to Trailhead: The trailhead is located on the campus of the California Polytechnic State University, better known as Cal Poly. To reach the trailhead, take Grand Avenue north from Monterey Street onto the Poly Campus. Be sure to purchase a parking permit if Cal Poly is in session. Continue straight until you reach a "T" intersection, Perimeter Road. Turn right here and follow the road up and just slightly over the hill to a stop sign, or until you reach Poly Canyon Road. Turn right here and park your car in the parking lot.

Trail Overview: This is another trail exploring the Poly Canyon area. The semiloop trail goes mostly along a farm road with a short section of actual trail. It starts with pleasant walk along Brizziolari Creek, explores the bottom of Poly Canyon, and finally climbs to a saddle dividing Poly Canyon and Stenner Creek Canyon. West Cuesta Ridge is the prominent backdrop for this hike. There are three other potential destinations for those wishing to explore this area in more detail. They are the Cal Poly Horse Unit, Stenner Creek Canyon, and the Poly Canyon Architectural Area.

Trail Description:

Poly Canyon Trailhead. From the parking lot we pass through an open gate surrounded by eucalyptus trees. The road quickly turns to dirt as it passes above the cattle unit and starts to wind its way into the canyon. We again enter a grove of eucalyptus with a

road to the right leading to the Poly dump. Just ahead is a short trail to our left leading down to Brizziolari Creek. If you cross the creek, you can take a less used trail to the wooden bridge. We will continue along the road reaching a

wooden bridge spanning Brizziolari Creek. Do not cross the bridge. Continue along the road, where just past the bridge is a rock arch leading into Poly Canyon architectural area. This trail goes up to the ridge and rejoins the main trail, but it is not well maintained. Our route continues along the road to the

Ranch Houses ahead and a gate. Pass through this gate then descend a short distance to another gate shaded by a large sycamore tree. The road continues straight, then rounds a bend to the right to reach a

road to the left. Turn left and climb 160 feet up the hill to another

road junction. Turn right here. At this point the trail starts to narrow as it contours the hill and passes through a

gate. A short climb offers us views of West Cuesta Ridge and Poly Canyon. The trail narrows and descends to a

wire gate beneath the oaks. From here, the trail starts its final climb to the saddle overlooking both Poly and Stenner Canyons. On top of the saddle, there is a cluster of

serpentine rocks, a good spot for a lunch or rest stop. Leaving the rocks behind, the trail continues along the fence line, rejoining the

Poly Canyon Road. If you wish to hike through Stenner Canyon, turn left at this point. To return to the parking lot, pass through the gate. Be sure to stay on the road, as the properties on both sides of this road are privately owned. Our trail turns right, downhill, rounding many bends before reaching a

gate with a corral. Continue along the road again through one more gate to reach the

road junction we climbed earlier. From this point retrace your steps along the road to the entrance of

Poly Canyon trailhead.

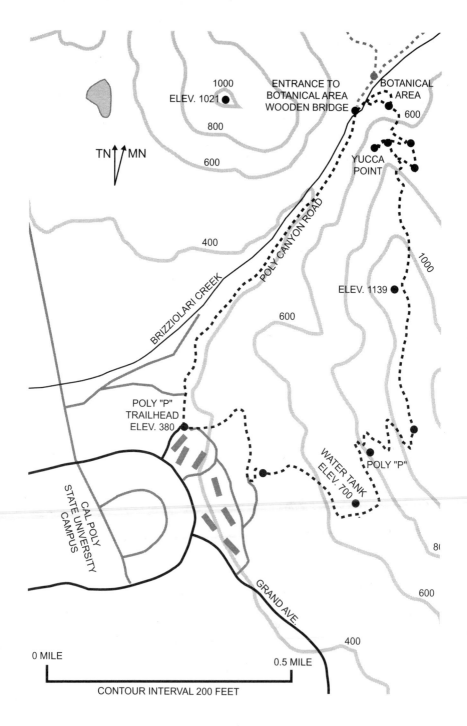

Poly "P"

Poly "P" Loop

Usage:	Hikers and Dogs
Fee:	Campus Parking Fee if Applicable
Distance:	2.9 Miles (Round Trip)
Elevation Gain/Loss:	+720/-720 Feet
Approx. Hiking Time:	2-3 Hours Round Trip
Hike Rating:	OModerate
USGS Maps:	San Luis Obispo

Best Time to Hike: All Year

Point On Route:	Distance from Starting Point Miles(Km)	Elevation
Entrance to Poly Canyon Trailhead	0.0 (0.0)	380
Road to Right	0.4 (0.6)	440
Wooden Bridge	0.7 (1.1)	480
East Canyon Trail Junction	0.9 (1.4)	640
Bob's Trail Junction	1.0 (1.6)	680
South Boundary Trail Junction	1.1 (1.8)	2580
Yucca Viewpoint Junction	1.2 (1.9)	860
Top of Ridge	1.5 (2.4)	1100
Cairns Trail down to "P"	1.8 (2.9)	1100
Base of Poly "P"	2.1 (3.4)	800
Water Tank	2.3 (3.7)	680
Locked Gate	2.5 (4.0)	480
Entrance to Poly Canyon	2.9 (4.7)	380

Directions to Trailhead: The trailhead is located on the campus of the California Polytechnic State University, better known as Cal Poly. To reach the trailhead, take Grand Ave north from Monterey Street onto the Poly Campus. Be sure to purchase a parking permit if Cal Poly is in session. Continue straight until you reach a "T" intersection, Perimeter Road. Turn right here and follow the road up and just slightly over the hill to a stop sign, or until you reach Poly Canyon Road. Turn right here and park your car in the parking lot.

Trail Overview: Though this trail is relatively short compared to others in the book, it is rated moderate because of the 700' elevation gain. This is a good year-round trail. With a moderate amount of effort, the hiker will be treated to some of the best views of San Luis Obispo, Cuesta Ridge and the Poly and Reservoir Canyons. Wildflowers flourish here in spring. This trail was partially built in the late 1980s by the California Conservation Corps (CCC). The trail on the face of the "P" was built in 1998 by the local chapter of the Sierra Club. The addition makes this an enjoyable loop trail.

Trail Description:

Poly Canyon Trailhead. From the parking lot we pass through an open gate surrounded by eucalyptus trees. The road quickly turns to dirt as it passes above the cattle unit and starts to wind its way into the canyon. We again enter a grove of eucalyptus with a

road to our right leading to the Poly dump. Just ahead is a short trail to our left leading down to Brizziolari Creek. If you cross the creek, you can take a less-used trail to the wooden bridge. We will continue along the road, reaching a

wooden bridge. The trail crosses the creek and enters the Cal Poly Botanical Area. Go right at the fork just past the bridge. The trail starts a steady and sometimes steep climb over a rocky trail. It first comes to

East Canyon Trail Junction. You can turn right here if you wish and rejoin the trail just ahead. We take the left fork, climbing to

Bob's Trail Junction. Turn right here, and walk about 100 yards to the

South Boundary Trail. Turn left here and continue up the hill. The trail, still climbing steeply, eventually comes to a rocky outcropping leading to the

Yucca Viewpoint Junction. Continue to the left, climbing to the

top of the ridge at 1100 feet. Make sure to take in the fine views along this ridge from San Luis Obispo to Morro Bay. Several of the Nine Sisters can be seen, including San Luis Mountain, Bishop Peak, Chumash Peak, Cerro Romauldo, and Hollister Peak. The trail now heads south along the ridge for 0.3 mile to a

cairn or large rock on the left as the trail swings right, then left, down a set of well-graded switchbacks. If you are going straight downhill, you missed the left turn. The trail continues its descent to a small open meadow,

then switches again to the

base of the Poly "P". From the "P", the trail traverses the hill and reaches the buried water tank. Follow the access road to a

locked gate. Just beyond the gate, follow the road left to the parking area, then make a right turn over a small rise before descending the final 100 feet and returning to the

Poly Canyon Trailhead.

ISLAY CREEK TRAIL

San Luis Obispo Other Areas

A few other public areas deserve mention here. For the most part, these are open spaces with few formal trails.

Islay Hill Open Space

Usage:	Hikers and Dogs on Leash
Fee:	None at this Time
Distance:	0.5 Mile (One Way)
Elevation Gain/Loss:	400 Feet
Approx. Hiking Time:	1 Hour
Hike Rating:	Easy
USGS Maps:	San Luis Obispo

Best Time to Hike: All Year

This trail climbs 400 feet, steeply near the top of the hill, and serves as a good, 45-minute workout. It also offers panoramic views of Edna Valley. The trail branches midway up the hill. The fork to the right leads straight up the hill over a long set of slippery stairs which will eventually be washed out completely, and is not recommended. Take the left fork, which contours the northeast side of the hill. Beware of loose dirt, and watch for poison oak at the top.

Directions to Trailhead:

The formal entrance to the Islay Hill Trail is found at the end of Sweetbay Road in the Arbors development. From Tank Farm Road, turn onto Wavertree and follow it to the end. Go left on Spanish Oaks and bear right onto Sweetbay, a short cul-de-sac by the railroad tracks.

Laguna Lake Park

Usage:	Hikers, Mountain Bikers and Dogs on Leash
Fee:	None at this Time
Distance:	1 Mile (Round Trip)
Elevation Gain/Loss:	40 Feet
Approx. Hiking Time:	1 Hour
Hike Rating:	Easy
USGS Maps:	San Luis Obispo

Best Time to Hike: All Year

Laguna Lake Park is located just off Madonna Road between Highway 101 and Los Osos Valley Road. This area offers many opportunities for exploration: walking along Laguna Lake itself; using the Spangler Exercise Trail; climbing the western slopes of San Luis Mountain; and access to the 40 acres north of Laguna Lake Park. There are a variety of wildflowers and many bird species that inhabit Laguna Lake and the surrounding area. While hiking this area be sure to take in the wonderful views of the Morros.

Directions to Trailhead:

From Highway 101 take the Madonna Road exit. Turn West towards Los Osos Valley Road. When you reach the post office, Laguna Lake Park is on the right hand side. Turn right at the light and park anywhere in the park to enjoy this beautiful area.

Prefumo Canyon

Usage:	Hikers, Mountain Bikers and Dogs on Leash
Fee:	None at this Time
Distance:	2.5 Miles (Round Trip)
Elevation Gain/Loss:	+700/-700 Feet
Approx. Hiking Time:	2-3 Hours
Hike Rating:	Moderate
USGS Maps:	San Luis Obispo

Best Time to Hike: All Year

Prefumo Canyon is the most recent addition to the City of San Luis Obispo Greenbelt. This 366-acre parcel hosts a wide variety of vegetation, some of which can be considered rare. This area can be explored by walking on one of the many mining roads that travel through the area. A short semi-loop is currently being constructed near the top of the ridge connecting to an old mine. The top offers great views of Los Osos Valley and the western slopes of San Luis Mountain. This area will eventually connect to Madonna Road.

Directions to Trailhead:

From Highway 101 take the Madonna Road exit and turn west towards Los Osos Valley Road. Head right on Los Osos Valley Road towards Los Osos. At Prefumo Canyon Road turn left. Drive along Prefumo Canyon road until you cross a concrete bridge (Prefumo Creek). A small parking area is planned, but for now park alongside the road and go through the piped gate on the left side (south) of the road.

Reservoir Canyon

Usage:	Hikers, Mountain Bikers and Dogs on Leash
Fee:	None at this Time
Distance:	1 Mile (One Way)
Elevation Gain/Loss:	200 Feet
Approx. Hiking Time:	1 Hour
Hike Rating:	Easy
USGS Maps:	San Luis Obispo

Best Time to Hike: All Year

Located on the outskirts of San Luis Obispo, this 80-acre area is great for
birding around a wetland pond, viewing wildlflowers, and taking a 1 mile hike
up reservoir canyon itself. Recent improvents have put in a couple of
bridges to ford San Luis Creek.

Directions to Trailhead:

To reach this area from San Luis Obispo, take Highway 101 North to
Reservoir Canyon Road. Turn right and drive to the end of the road. Park in
the dirt parking area. Please heed the many "No Trespassing" signs. It is
easy inadvertently to cross onto private property.

Please note: Leaving Reservoir Canyon to head south on U.S. 101 requires a
dangerous left turn across both lanes of traffic. It is suggested, instead, to
turn right onto 101 and drive north about ½ mile, where a U-turn is possible
from a left-hand turn lane.

South Hills Open Space

Usage:	Hikers and Dogs on Leash
Fee:	None at this Time
Distance:	1.5 Miles (Round Trip)
Elevation Gain/Loss:	500 Feet
Approx. Hiking Time:	1-2 Hours
Hike Rating:	Easy
USGS Maps:	San Luis Obispo

Best Time to Hike: All Year

Located behind Stoneridge Estates and Meadow Park, this area is uniquely different from other parts of San Luis Obispo. There are no formal trails, but rather many well-defined paths leading to overlooks of the city and Edna Valley. You will also find lichen-covered stone outcroppings that continue to evolve with passing time. For the adventurous hiker, a 1.5 mile loop is an option. Wear sturdy shoes.

Directions to Trailhead:

From South Street in San Luis Obispo, turn onto Exposition Drive and look for the South Hills Open Space sign on the right hand side (west) of Exposition Drive, at Corrida.

Stenner Creek Road

Usage:	Hikers, Horses, Mountain Bikers and Dogs on Leash
Fee:	None at this Time
Distance:	2.0 Miles (One Way)
Elevation Gain/Loss:	200 feet
Approx. Hiking Time:	1 Hour
Hike Rating:	Easy
USGS Maps:	San Luis Obispo

Best Time to Hike: All Year

This is not a formal trail, but rather a walk, two miles one way. It takes us to the Old White Ranch House at the end of the road and explores Stenner Creek and Cal Poly property. The highlights are a year-round stream and wonderful vistas of West Cuesta Ridge, as well as the old train trestle, which is said to have been built from the same steel used in the construction of the Eiffel Tower in Paris.

Directions to Trailhead:

To reach Stenner Creek from San Luis Obispo, take Highway 1 North to Stenner Creek Road. This is the first right past Highland Drive in San Luis Obispo. Turn right and drive one mile to the trail trestle. Park along the road.

Terrace Hill

Usage:	Hikers, Horses, Mountain Bikers and Dogs on Leash
Fee:	None at this Time
Distance:	0.1 Mile (One Way)
Elevation Gain/Loss:	150 Feet
Approx. Hiking Time:	1/2 Hour
Hike Rating:	Easy
USGS Maps:	San Luis Obispo

Best Time to Hike: All Year

Terrace Hill, at elevation 501 feet, is one of the smaller Morros. It offers some of the best views of San Luis Obispo and the surrounding area. There is no formal parking area. A pedestrian gate is located on Bishop Street just past Augusta Street on the right-hand side of the road. This is a popular hike with area residents.

Directions to Trailhead:

To reach Terrace hill take Johnson Avenue to Bishop Street. Turn west onto Bishop Street, toward the railroad tracks. After the stop sign at Augusta Street, continue straight about 100 yards to the pedestrian gate leading to Terrace Hill.

Los Padres National Forest

Dec 14 '88
on Cabrillo Peak

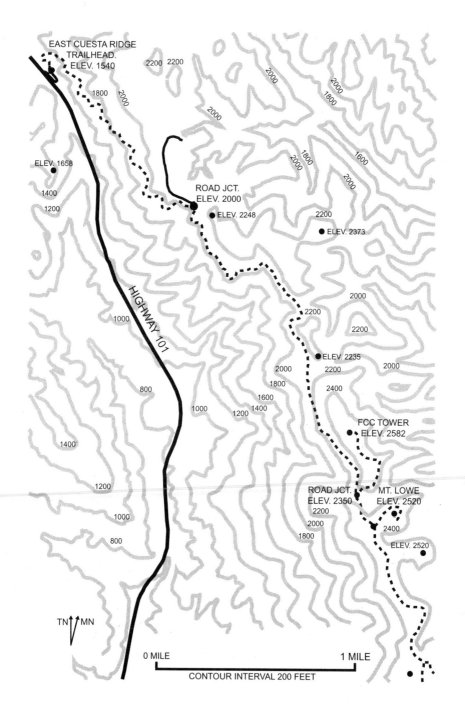

East Cuesta Ridge

East Cuesta Ridge

Usage:	Hikers, Mountain Bikers and Dogs
Fee:	None
Distance:	4 Miles (One Way)
Elevation Gain/Loss:	1060 Feet
Approx. Hiking Time:	5 Hours Round Trip
Hike Rating:	Moderate
USGS Maps:	Lopez Mountain

Best Time to Hike: All Year

Point On Route:	Distance from Starting Point Miles(Km)	Elevation
East Cuesta Ridge Trailhead	0.0 (0.0)	1520
Cattle Guard	0.9 (1.4)	1920
Santa Margarita Ranch Road Junction	1.5 (2.4)	2020
Old East Cuesta Ridge Trail to Helicopter Pad	2.4 (3.8)	2100
Road Junction	3.5 (5.6)	2400
Radio Facility Hilltop	4.0 (6.4)	2580

Directions to Trailhead: This trailhead is only accessible from northbound lanes of Highway 101. From San Luis Obispo take 101 North to the Cuesta Summit, which may be marked by a sign reading "Elevation 1522 feet." Go another 150 yards north of the summit to a paved truck pullout. Turn right here, go up the narrow unmarked road, and park off the dirt road. Parking in the pullout itself is subject to a fine.

Trail Overview: The trail is a well maintained dirt road with little vehicle use. It accesses the many repeater stations atop Cuesta Ridge. It offers many views of San Luis Obispo, Reservoir Canyon, the Morros and the South Coast along the Oceano Dunes to Mussel Rock. To the north you can see Morro Rock and Estero Bay. The area has recovered nicely from the 1985 Las Pilitas fire and the Highway 41 fire in 1994. Vegetation includes knobcone pines, manzanita, madrone trees, live oaks and a variety of wildflowers.

Trail Description:

East Cuesta Ridge Trailhead. Our trail takes us over a locked gate, then climbs steadily along the access road. The road starts off in a northerly direction, then soon makes a 180 degree turn and continues in a southerly direction for the remainder of the hike. The first 1.5 miles of this trail run across private property until it enters the Los Padres National Forest. We quickly leave highway noise behind as we wind our way up the ridge. At 0.9 mile, we enter a shady live oak forest, then cross a

cattle guard. The trail breaks out into open, impressive views of San Luis Obispo and Reservoir Canyon. Making a left turn we reach the

Santa Margarita Ranch Road junction with a cable across the road. This road is on private property. We bear to the right, crossing a second cattle guard into the Los Padres National Forest. From here the trail is fairly level for the next 0.7 mile and offers panoramic views of San Luis Obispo and the south coast. At the 2.4 mile point we come to what used to be the

Old East Cuesta Ridge Trail. This is now completely overgrown and is not slated to be maintained or cleared. The trail again starts to climb for another mile until you reach the first of many

road junctions ahead. To reach Lopez Canyon, continue straight for another 1.1 mile to reach the start of the trail. Otherwise, turn left here. We can see Mt. Lowe, with its radio tower, immediately to the right. A short distance after the turn, we get our first views to the east. Santa Margarita Ranch and a lush new forest are immediately below, and the Black Mountain Radar Station can be seen off in the distance. The road is surrounded on both sides by new pine trees. We come to the

radio facility and the end of our journey. If you skirt the facility on the right, you will find a large level spot for lunch and views of San Luis Obispo, Oceano Dunes and Morro Bay.

UPPER HAZARD
CANYON TRAIL

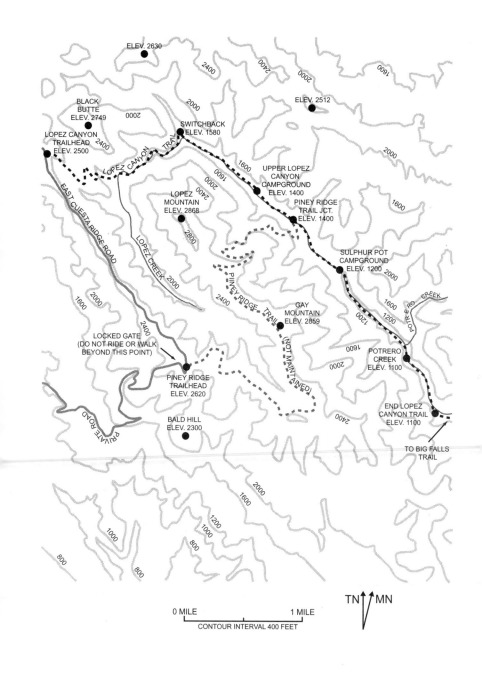

ELEV. 2630

BLACK
BUTTE
ELEV. 2749

2400

2400

2000

2000

1600

ELEV. 2512

LOPEZ CANYON
TRAILHEAD
ELEV. 2500

2000

2400

LOPEZ CANYON TRAIL

SWITCHBACK
ELEV. 1580

2000

1600

1600

UPPER LOPEZ
CANYON
CAMPGROUND
ELEV. 1400

2000

EAST CUESTA RIDGE ROAD

LOPEZ MOUNTAIN
ELEV. 2868

2400

2000

2800

PINEY RIDGE
TRAIL JCT.
ELEV. 1400

1600

LOPEZ CREEK

2000

PINEY RIDGE TRAIL

SULPHUR POT
CAMPGROUND
ELEV. 1200

2000

1600

2400

POTRERO CREEK

1600

1200

1200

LOCKED GATE
(DO NOT RIDE OR WALK
BEYOND THIS POINT)

GAY
MOUNTAIN
ELEV. 2859

(NOT MAINTAINED)

1600

PINEY RIDGE
TRAILHEAD
ELEV. 2620

2000

2000

POTRERO
CREEK
ELEV. 1100

PRIVATE ROAD

BALD HILL
ELEV. 2300

2400

END LOPEZ
CANYON TRAIL
ELEV. 1100

TO BIG FALLS
TRAIL

2000

1600

1200

1000

800

1000

800

800

0 MILE   1 MILE

CONTOUR INTERVAL 400 FEET

TN   MN

Lopez Canyon

Lopez Canyon

Usage:	Hikers, Horses and Dogs
Fee:	AdventurePass
Distance:	5.3 Miles (One Way)
Elevation Gain/Loss:	-1400 Feet
Approx. Hiking Time:	4 – 6 Hours (Down and Back)
Hike Rating:	Moderately Strenuous
USGS Maps:	Lopez Mountain

Best Time to Hike: Winter, Spring, Late Fall

Point On Route:	Distance from Starting Point Miles(Km)	Elevation
Lopez Canyon Trailhead	0.0 (0.0)	2500
Lopez Creek	1.3 (2.1)	1580
Upper Lopez Camp	3.1 (5.0)	1400
Sulphur Pot Camp	4.3 (6.9)	1200
Lopez Canyon Road	5.3 (8.5)	1100

Directions to Trailhead: This trailhead is only accessible from northbound lanes of Highway 101. From San Luis Obispo take 101 North to the Cuesta Summit, which may be marked by a sign reading "Elevation 1522 Feet." Look for a paved truck pullout 150 yards north of the summit. Turn right here; go up the narrow unmarked road, and park off the road. Parking in the pullout itself is subject to a fine. Unfortunately, you can no longer drive to the trailhead. Instead, you will have to hike, bike or horseback ride the dirt road 4.6 miles to the Lopez Canyon Trailhead. Bikes must be left at the trailhead.

Trail Overview: Our trail descends 1400 feet through Lopez Canyon, a beautiful expanse of wilderness in the Santa Lucia Mountains. The large number of plant varieties, some of them rare, make this area a botanist's paradise. The trail conditions vary depending on when it was last maintained. The first half of the trail is relatively free of poison oak, but once in the canyon, poison oak can be quite thick and unavoidable. Numerous creek crossings mean wet feet in the rainy season. There are two camps along the trail, Upper Lopez Campground, and Sulphur Pot Campground. Upper Lopez Campground is easy to find. There are no longer any tables or potable water at any of these campsites. All water must be hauled in or filtered from Lopez Creek. If a shuttle trip is planned follow the directions to reach the south end

153

of the Big Falls trail, then continue up Lopez Canyon Road 2.5 miles to the Lopez Canyon Trailhead. Depending on the condition of Lopez Canyon Road, one may have to leave the shuttle vehicle closer to the Big Falls Trail than expected, making the trip that much longer.

Trail Description:

Lopez Canyon Trailhead. Our trail starts down along a ridge with chaparral on both sides. After the end of the ridge, a series of switchbacks descend through a lush forest of madrone and bay trees before we reach

Lopez Creek. The trail stays to the left of the creek for a short while. On one location a spring seeps directly from porous rocks on the hillside. The canyon narrows and we cross the stream a few times before leaving the stream below. The trail rounds a point with good views down Lopez Canyon before descending to Lopez Creek again. Remember this spot—it is easy to miss the sharp switchback on the return trip. Once on the canyon floor, the trail crosses an open meadow. In addition, the vegetation becomes denser as we head down the canyon. Once across the meadow the trail follows the left side of the canyon. Huge bay and oaks trees tower above. There may be a few stream crossings and plenty of poison oak depending on trail conditions. Reaching

Upper Lopez Campground, we find a large level spot, free of poison oak. All the tables have been removed or used as firewood. This is a pleasant one during the summer months, but a cold campground in winter. Leaving the campground, we cross the stream several times. 0.3 mile past the camp we come to an old jeep road on the right. This road is no longer maintained. Continue straight downstream with many more creek crossings ahead. One mile past the jeep road junction,

Sulphur Pot Campground may be seen on the left side of the canyon. The campground is reached by a taking short side trail up the hill. The camp is named for the hydrogen sulfide gas released from moss covered seeps where the stream has cut to bedrock. Leaving Sulphur Pot behind, the trail crosses Lopez Creek several more times. 0.9 mile past the camp, Potrero Creek comes in from the left. A sandstone uplift creates a swimming hole and what appears to be a dancing waterfall. The pool may be filled in due to heavy rains. This area was used as a squatter's camp on occasion. 0.1 one mile past this creek we come technically to

Lopez Canyon Road. This is a poorly maintained road. During wet weather you may have to travel another 2.5 miles to the Big Falls Trailhead to reach a shuttle vehicle. Otherwise retrace your steps 5.3 miles back to the trailhead.

Big Falls

Usage:	Hikers, Horses and Dogs
Fee:	Adventure Pass
Distance:	3.0 Miles (One Way)
Elevation Gain/Loss:	+1300/-50 Feet (One Way)
Approx. Hiking Time:	2-3 Hours (One Way)
Hike Rating:	Moderately Strenuous
USGS Maps:	Lopez Mountain

Best Time to Hike: Winter, Spring, Late Fall

Point On Route:	Distance from Starting Point Miles(Km)	Elevation
Big Falls Trailhead	0.0 (0.0)	790
Lower Big Falls	0.4 (0.6)	843
Big Falls Narrows	1.0 (1.6)	1050
Upper Big Falls Junction	1.2 (1.9)	1100
Upper Big Falls	1.5 (2.4)	1180
Saddle	2.8 (4.5)	1830
Hi Mountain Road	3.0 (4.8)	2010

Directions to Trailhead: From San Luis Obispo, allow at least one hour to reach the trailhead. Once in Arroyo Grande, drive 2 miles east on Huasna Road. Bear left onto Lopez Drive, and go 8 miles to Lopez Lake. Drive along the lake, after crossing the bridge just before Lopez Lake Entrance Station, then turn right onto Arroyo Grande-Pozo Road, also known as Hi Mountain Road. Go 0.8 mile to Lopez Canyon Road. Turn left and drive 7.2 miles over two ridges, passing French (Boy Scout) Camp and Lopez Canyon Conference Grounds. The road then turns to dirt. The Little Falls Trailhead is marked by a small, poorly visible sign on the right. Then drive another 2 miles to the Big Falls Trailhead. It is on the right side of the road and also hard to see.

Be aware that entering Lopez Canyon from this direction may be difficult during high water and winter months. The road is dirt for much of the way and crosses Lopez Creek many times. It may be better to access this trail via the Rinconada Trail. Alternatively, cross the Salinas River near Pozo, drive 4 miles to the summit, and take the road 6 miles to the right to the upper trailhead area. These roads are impassable during wet weather.

Trail Overview: This trail offers much for the hiker: forests, oak woodland and open hillsides, as well as two waterfalls, one at the lower end of the trail and one about halfway up. In spring there are abundant wildflowers, the streams are running full, and there are a few swimming holes to cool off in on a warm day. Beware of slippery rocks and poison oak.

It is possible to make several different trips while visiting the two falls in the area. One is the 12-mile loop starting at Big or Little Falls Trailhead, another takes the Rinconada Trail to reach Upper Big Falls. All three trails make a 16-mile loop, or, for a brief outing, go to the lower falls for a swim.

Trail Description:

Big Falls Trail. Our trail starts by crossing Lopez Creek, which can be a wet ford. We first follow the left side of the creek, then cross it, continuing on the right-hand side by large bay trees, sycamores and oaks. We reach the

Lower Big Falls Junction. The left fork goes to the pool at the base of the falls. The right fork continues up to the top of the falls itself. A steep goat path leads to the top. Once over the falls, the trail enters a deep canyon with the creek to our left. The sounds of running water make this trail a delight. We then cross the creek continuing on the left side of the stream to Big Falls Narrows, a rock gateway with good views up the canyon. Watch for an occasional snake. The trail descends again to the creek before crossing it one more time. Just ahead is the

Upper Big Falls Junction. The left fork takes you to the base of the waterfall. The large pool can serve as a welcome foot bath. Watch for poison oak. The right fork is hard to see, as it is actually a switchback to the right. It gradually climbs to the top of

Upper Big Falls, where we find the best swimming holes along the creek. They are in the open sun and are about 4-6 feet deep in spots. Look for salamanders and turtles. Leaving the ponds, the trail continues up along the stream, crossing to the left side, then finally crossing to the right over a rock ledge. We enter an oak woodland forest as we start our climb out of the canyon on two or three gradual switchbacks. The trail then climbs steeply for 0.2 mile before it again levels out. We are now following a small creek up the canyon. Crossing the stream, we start our final ascent over several well-graded switchbacks through a delightful meadow to the saddle above. Once at the

Saddle, we turn to the right, east, ascending slightly and reaching

Hi Mountain Road at an elevation 2250'. You can either continue along the road returning via Little Falls, or retrace your steps back to the Big Falls trailhead.

LOWER FALLS.
BIG FALLS CANYON — SANTA LUCIA WILDERNESS

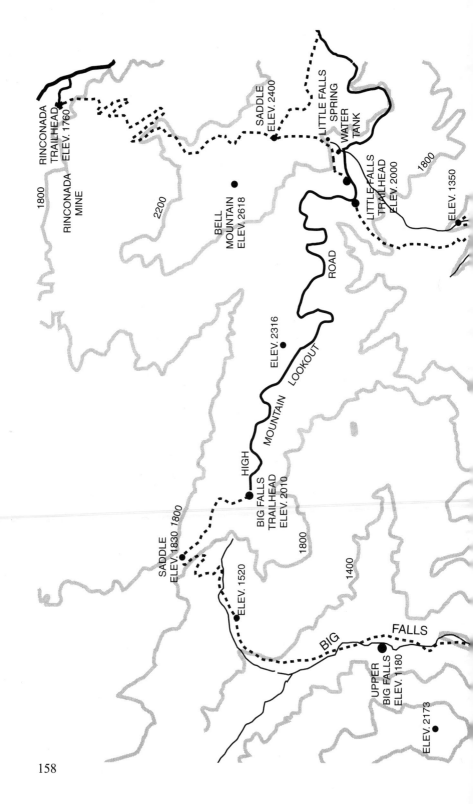

RINCONADA TRAILHEAD ELEV. 1760

RINCONADA MINE

1800

2200

BELL MOUNTAIN ELEV. 2618

SADDLE ELEV. 2400

LITTLE FALLS SPRING

WATER TANK

LITTLE FALLS TRAILHEAD ELEV. 2000

ELEV. 1350

1800

ROAD

ELEV. 2316

HIGH MOUNTAIN LOOKOUT

BIG FALLS TRAILHEAD ELEV. 2010

SADDLE ELEV. 1830 1800

ELEV. 1520

1800

1400

BIG FALLS

UPPER BIG FALLS ELEV. 1180

ELEV. 2173

Big Falls/Little Falls/Rinconada

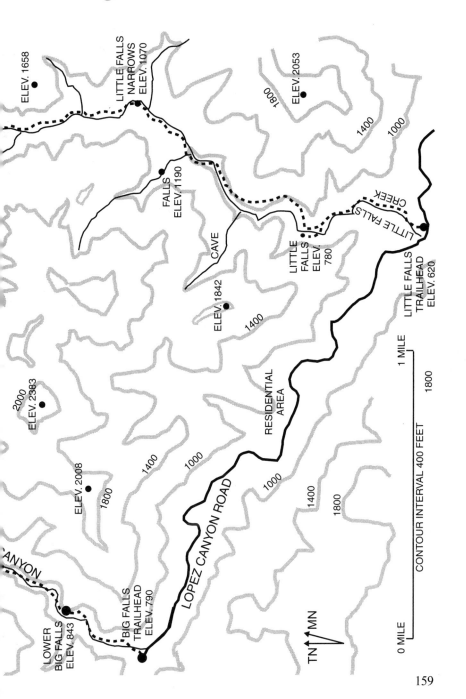

ELEV. 1658

LITTLE FALLS
NARROWS
ELEV. 1070

ELEV. 2053

1800

1400

1000

FALLS
ELEV. 1190

CAVE

LITTLE FALLS CREEK

LITTLE
FALLS
ELEV.
780

ELEV. 1842

1400

LITTLE FALLS
TRAILHEAD
ELEV. 620

1 MILE

2000
ELEV. 2383

RESIDENTIAL
AREA

1000

1800

ELEV. 2008

1400

1000

1000

1400

1800

1800
CONTOUR INTERVAL 400 FEET

LOPEZ CANYON ROAD

CANYON

LOWER
BIG FALLS
ELEV. 843

BIG FALLS
TRAILHEAD
ELEV. 790

TN MN

0 MILE

Little Falls

Usage:	Hikers, Horses and Dogs
Fee:	Adventure Pass Fee
Distance:	2.8 Miles One Way
Elevation Gain/loss:	+1350 Feet
Approx. Hiking Time:	4 - 5 Hours
Hike Rating:	Moderately Strenuous
USGS Maps:	Santa Margarita Lake

Best Time to Hike: Winter, Spring, Late Fall

Point On Route:	Distance from Starting Point Miles(Km)	Elevation
Little Falls Trailhead	0.0 (0.0)	620
Junction Little Falls	0.4 (0.6)	700
Top of Little Falls	0.8 (1.3)	800
Stream Crossing	1.3 (2.0)	1000
Little Falls Narrows	1.4 (2.2)	1070
Creek Crossing	1.9 (3.0)	1350
Hi Mountain Road	2.8 (4.5)	2080

Directions to Trailhead: Allow one hour for the 29-mile drive to the trailhead from San Luis Obispo. From Arroyo Grande drive two miles east on Huasna Road. Bear left onto Lopez Drive, and drive 8 miles to Lopez Lake. Drive along the lake. After crossing the bridge just before Lopez Lake entrance turn right onto Hi Mountain Road. Go 0.8 mile to Upper Lopez Canyon Road. Turn left and drive 7.2 miles over two ridges passing French (Boy Scout) Camp and Lopez Canyon Conference Grounds. The road then turns to dirt. Drive the last 1.5 miles to the Little Falls trailhead. The trail is marked by a small sign on the right.

Entering Lopez Canyon from this direction may be difficult during high water and winter months, and a high clearance vehicle is recommended. The road is dirt for much of the way and crosses Lopez Creek several times. It is possible to access this trail via the Rinconada Trail. Alternatively, two other options are available. One is to cross the Salinas River near Pozo, drive 4 miles to the summit, then take the road to the right to the upper trailhead area. The other option is to hike in from the Rinconada Mine trailhead, which goes over a ridge and ends at Hi Mountain Road about 100 yards west of Little Falls upper trailhead.

Trail Overview: The Little Falls trail ascends 1350 feet, climbing through a forested canyon with a small but spectacular, and well hidden, waterfall. The fall is about 50 feet high, with a large pool at its base. A rich landscape of oak woodland, sycamore, coastal sage scrub and streamside vegetation thrive along the trail. In spring numerous wildflowers are found in the canyon, including scarlet larkspur, prickly phlox, black sage, monkey flowers, lupine and poison oak. Hi Mountain Road offers great views of the Santa Lucia Wilderness. For a loop trip, hike west to the Big Falls Trail, then descend to Lopez Canyon.

Trail Description:

Little Falls Trailhead. The trail starts adjacent to Lopez Canyon Road and quickly enters an oak forest, opening up to a small meadow. A sign explains the rules when entering the Santa Lucia Wilderness. Beware of poison oak when the trail crosses Little Falls creek two more times before reaching the

Little Falls Trail Junction. To go to the falls, take the left fork of the trail a short distance along the stream to a small pool shaded by large sycamore trees. Little Falls is another 200 feet upstream. Be prepared for wet feet when accessing the base of Little Falls. To continue to Hi Mountain Road, cross the stream a third time and start a steep ascent along what appears to be an old mining road to the

top of Little Falls. The trail then levels out a bit before starting another steep climb. After the second ascent, the trail levels out once more before dropping slightly to cross

Little Falls Creek again. Once across the stream the trail climbs slowly along the stream. Eventually, the canyon starts to narrow before rounding a rocky bend in the canyon know as

Little Falls Narrows. This is a wet crossing during winter months and after spring storms. Be sure to look for the many newts that inhabit this area. Once across the narrows, the trails climbs a bit more steeply through oak and sycamore forest reaching our last

stream crossing before starting a 0.9-mile ascent to Hi Mountain Road. The trail breaks out of the forest into thick chaparral, which can be very hot at any time of the year. Once at

Hi Mountain Road, be sure to take in the scenery and a well-deserved rest.

Rinconada Mine

Usage:	Hikers, Horses, Mountain Bikes and Dogs
Fee:	Adventure Pass Fee
Distance:	2 Miles One Way
Elevation Gain/Loss:	+600/ -300 Feet
Approx. Hiking Time:	2 - 3 Hours
Hike Rating:	Moderate
USGS Maps:	Santa Margarita Lake

Best Time to Hike: Winter, Spring, Late Fall

Point On Route:	Distance from Starting Point Miles(Km)	Elevation
Rinconada Trailhead	0.0 (0.0)	1740
Leave Road/Saddle	0.2 (0.3)	1840
Return to Fire Road	0.8 (1.3)	2160
Motor Vehicle Stop	1.3 (2.1)	2360
Saddle at top of hill	1.4 (2.2)	2380
Hi Mountain Lookout Road Trailhead	1.8 (2.9)	2080

Directions to Trailhead: Take the Santa Margarita (Hwy. 58) exit on US 101 and turn east toward Santa Margarita. Turn right on Hwy. 58. At the junction of Pozo Road and Hwy. 58, follow the signs to Santa Margarita Lake (Pozo Road). Drive approximately 7 miles to the Santa Margarita Lake turnoff. Continue straight on Pozo Road for another 3 miles. You will see a sign marking the Rinconada Trailhead. Turn right here and drive up the dirt road to the trailhead parking area. If you go over the top of the ridge on Pozo Road, you have gone too far. The trailhead is immediately to the east of the parking area.

Trail Overview: The Rinconada Trail is a recent addition to the Los Padres National Forest trail system. It allows much easier access to Big Falls and Little Falls Trails without the long, rough drive from Pozo over Hi Mountain Lookout Road. You can usually walk this trail faster than you can drive to the other end. This trail is a favorite of horseback riders accessing the area.

The trail itself is quite scenic as it ascends the side of Bell Mountain. It crosses oak woodlands, traverses through dense chaparral, and passes by several mines on both sides. A short semiloop of about 5.5 miles can also be made from this trailhead.

Trail Description:

Rinconada Trailhead. The trail, an old mine road, begins adjacent to the parking area next to the forest service signs. We cross two seeps before starting our climb. Take the right road up the hill when you reach an intersection a short distance along the trail. The left road deadends. Our route climbs steeply for about 100 yards, then turns left, to a trail sign. The trail

leaves the main road, then traverses an open meadow. At the end of the meadow, it switchbacks up the hill as we start our ascent of Bell Mountain. We quickly leave the oaks behind and climb into thick chaparral. Along the way one can see a wide variety of wildflowers: Indian warriors, chaparral currant, virgin bower, star lilies, and ceanothus. The trail climbs 300' along four switchbacks before

returning to the main fire road. Be sure to look around, as you will see the Black Mountain Radar Station across the valley to the north and the back side of the Santa Margarita Crags to the west. Once on the main road the trail climbs another 100' before it levels out. Watch for trail signs, as there are many old mining roads which lead in the wrong direction. Continuing along the old road, we come to a trail junction and a motor vehicle stop. Here you can take either trail as they rejoin 100 yards ahead, at the

top of the saddle. The views are Bell Mountain to the west, Lopez Canyon to the south and Pine Mountain Range to the east. Looking north we see Pozo Valley and Black Mountain Radar Station. At the saddle we can make a semiloop hike or to continue directly to Hi Mountain Lookout Road. The semiloop trip description can be found below. Continuing along the Rinconada Trail look for a large cairn (pile of rocks) with a trail sign stuck in it. Descend this steep rocky mine road to an open meadow. Once at the meadow continue straight down the main road. The other roads lead to several spots where Little Falls Springs originates. The trail now rounds a bend and Hi Mountain Lookout road comes into view. Follow the trail another one-tenth of a mile to reach

Hi Mountain Lookout Road. Little Falls Trailhead is 100 yards to the right.

Semiloop Trail Description: For a semiloop trip, take the old road to the east (left) through an open meadow of oaks, then along the ridgeline for about 0.5 mile until you connect to Hi Mountain Lookout Road. Along the ridge you will get splendid views of Pozo Valley and the mountains to the north. These include La Panza Range and Machesna Wilderness to the east. This walk is easy and enjoyable. Once at Hi Mountain Lookout Road we can retrace our steps, or turn right to follow Hi Mountain Lookout Road to the Rinconada Trail for another pleasant walk. Traveling along Hi Mountain Lookout Road, one gets excellent views of Little Falls and Lopez Canyon. After 0.8 mile you will reach the end of Rinconada Trail. Turn right again and follow the trail back to your starting point, the Rinconada Trailhead.

LOPEZ CANYON
FROM BLACK BUTTE, O
SANTA LUCIA
WILDERNESS

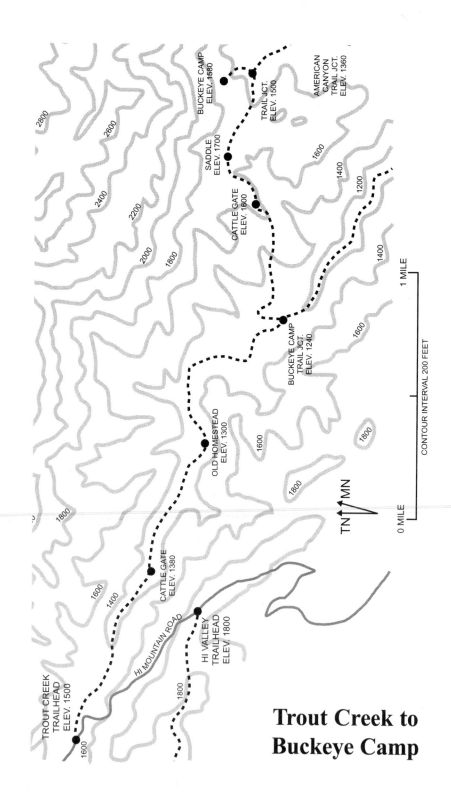

Trout Creek to Buckeye Camp

BUCKEYE CAMP ELEV. 1580

TRAIL JCT. ELEV. 1500

AMERICAN CANYON TRAIL JCT. ELEV. 1360

SADDLE ELEV. 1700

CATTLE GATE ELEV. 1600

BUCKEYE CAMP TRAIL JCT. ELEV. 1240

OLD HOMESTEAD ELEV. 1300

CATTLE GATE ELEV. 1380

HI VALLEY TRAILHEAD ELEV. 1800

HI MOUNTAIN ROAD

TROUT CREEK TRAILHEAD ELEV. 1500

TN MN

0 MILE 1 MILE

CONTOUR INTERVAL 200 FEET

2800 2600 2400 2200 2000 1800 1600 1400 1200

Trout Creek to Buckeye Camp

Usage:	Hikers, Horses and Dogs
Fee:	Adventure Pass
Distance:	4.0 miles (One Way)
Elevation Gain/Loss:	-460, +520 Feet
Approx. Hiking Time:	4-6 Hours
Hike Rating:	Moderate
USGS Maps:	Santa Margarita Lake, Caldwell Mesa

Best Time to Hike: Winter, Spring, Late Fall

Point On Route:	Distance from Starting Point Miles(Km)	Elevation
Trout Creek Trailhead	0.0 (0.0)	1500
Cattle Gate	1.0 (1.6)	1380
Old Homestead	1.8 (3.0)	1300
Buckeye Camp Trail Junction	2.5 (4.0)	1240
Cattle Gate	3.3 (5.2)	1600
Saddle	3.5 (5.5)	1700
Trail Junction	3.9 (6.3)	1500
Buckeye Camp	4.0 (6.5)	1540

Directions to Trailhead: Take the Santa Margarita (Hwy 58) exit from US 101 and turn east toward Santa Margarita. Turn right on Hwy 58. At the junction with Pozo Road and Hwy. 58, follow the signs to Santa Margarita Lake (Pozo Road). Drive approximately 7 miles to the Santa Margarita Lake turnoff. Continue straight on Pozo Road to Pozo, another 11 miles. Turn right onto Hi Mountain Lookout Road, in front of the Ranger Station. Drive 1 mile to the Salinas River. Cross the river and ascend the road for 4 miles to junction of Hi Mountain and Hi Mountain Lookout Road. Continue straight down the hill approximately 1.2 miles, crossing two small streams. Watch for a small pullout to the left, and possibly a trailhead sign. If you start climbing again on this road you have gone too far. This road is impassable in wet weather.

Trail Overview: This delightful trail follows Trout Creek for 2.5 miles and crosses it several times before it makes a sharp left turn to rise to the Garcia Wilderness Boundary. It is highlighted by oaks and grey pines, wildflowers

167

and many picnic spots. Portions of this creek run all year round allowing it to support fish as well. Be aware there are sections of this trail where poison oak may be unavoidable.

Trail Description:

Trout Creek Trailhead. Our trail begins on the south side of the stream. Immediately upon starting out you will find the Trout Creek Trail sign. Continue to the first of many stream crossings to an open meadow, sometimes filled with shooting stars. Just a bit further along, we cross a tributary followed by another creek crossing. Look for the trail on the other side—the boulders make finding it a bit difficult. Reaching the 1-mile point we come to a

cattle gate. Be sure to close the gate behind you. We continue to meander downstream, crossing Trout Creek several more times before coming to a large meadow. On the left will be some prickly pear cactus, and to the right a large oak. One of its branches seems especially made for sitting. From the looks of the area, this may have been an old cowboy camp or

old homestead. This makes a great place for a picnic lunch. The trail then crosses the creek two more times. It continues above the creek with the hillside on the left. We descend to creek level entering an oak grove. Look carefully, as the

Buckeye Camp Trail Junction is just ahead and takes a sharp left turn up the hill. Continuing straight along the exisiting trail will take the hiker to a fence and onto private property. Once you have found the trail to the left, climb to an open meadow and a Forest Service sign. You are now entering the Garcia Wilderness. The trail descends into a small gully then climbs out as we round the knoll coming to a

cattle gate. Pass through this gate, then climb a switchback for more views. The chaparral may get thick here as we continue to Buckeye Camp. Traveling down one more hill and up another we come to a

saddle bordered by large oak trees. The view to the left is Garcia Mountain. Across the valley is a high plateau where Caldwell Mesa and Bonnet Rock are located. The trail descends again to another meadow, then to a small stream crossing. Watch for the (faint)

trail junction just past the stream. It may or may not be marked. Continue straight another 0.1 mile to

Buckeye Camp itself. Buckeye Camp is heavily shaded under large oaks and bay trees, though buckeye trees are nowhere to be seen. It makes a good lunch spot and a nice place to cool off. At the camp there is a fire pit and running spring water. There may be a wilderness toilet nearby as well. Note the large boulders of pudding stone behind the camp.

If you are planning to continue to American Canyon, see that trip description (*American Canyon to Buckeye Camp*) for further information.

HIKERS ON THE TRAIL — HI MTN. RIDGE — SANTA LUCIA WILDERNESS

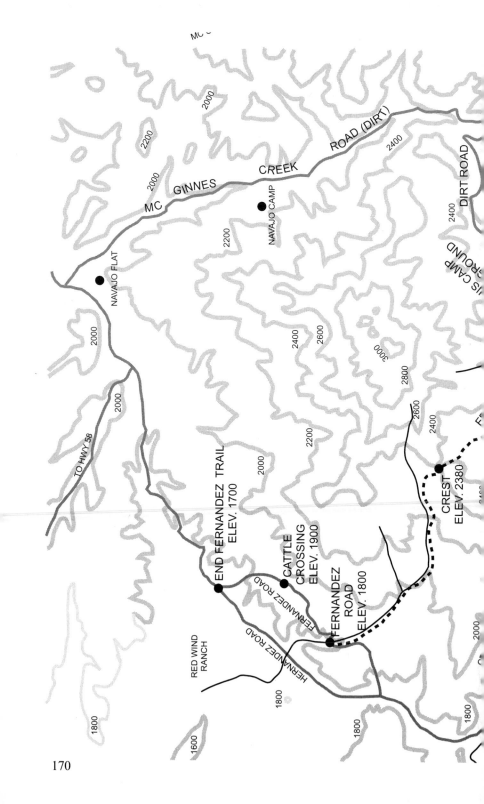

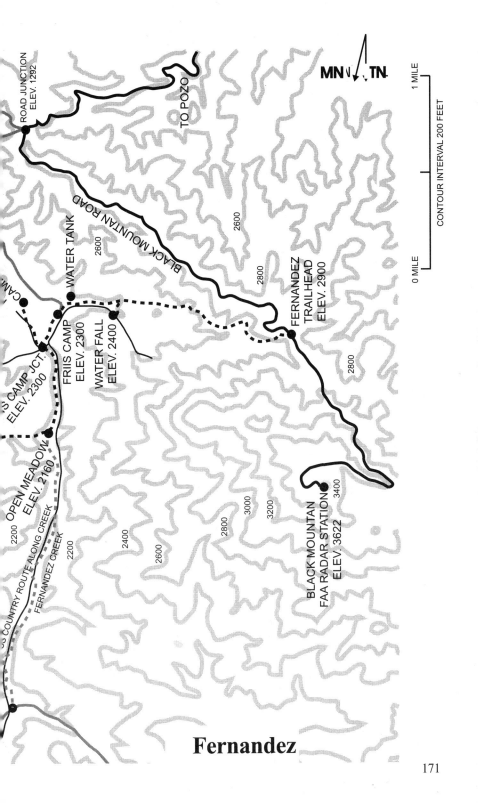

ROAD JUNCTION
ELEV. 1292

TO POZO

MN TN.

CONTOUR INTERVAL 200 FEET

1 MILE

0 MILE

BLACK MOUNTAIN ROAD

WATER TANK

2600

2600

2800

2800

2800

FERNANDEZ
TRAILHEAD
ELEV. 2900

CAMP

FRIIS CAMP
ELEV. 2300

WATER FALL
ELEV. 2400

'S CAMP JCT.
ELEV. 2300

OPEN MEADOW
ELEV. 2160

2200

2200

2200

2400

2600

2800

3000

3200

3400

BLACK MOUNTAIN
FAA RADAR STATION
ELEV. 3622

CROSS COUNTRY ROUTE ALONG CREEK

FERNANDEZ CREEK

Fernandez

171

Fernandez

Usage: Hikers, Horses, Mountain Bikers and Dogs
Fee: Adventure Pass
Distance: 5.8 Miles (One Way), 10.5-Mile Semiloop (Cross-Country)
Elevation Gain/Loss: +200/–1400 (One Way)
Approx. Hiking Time: 2-3 hours (One Way)
Hike Rating: Moderate
USGS Maps: Camatta Ranch

Best Time to Hike: Winter, Spring, Late Fall

Point On Route:	Distance from Starting Point Miles(Km)	Elevation
Fernandez Trailhead	0.0 (0.0)	2900
Waterfall	1.4 (2.2)	2400
Friis Camp	1.7 (2.7)	2300
Friis Camp Junction	1.8 (2.8)	2280
Meadow	2.5 (4.0)	2160
Crest	3.1 (5.0)	2380
Fernandez Road	4.3 (6.9)	1800
End Fernandez Trail	5.8 (9.3)	1700

Directions to Trailhead: Take Highway 101 to the Santa Margarita exit and turn east on Highway 58. Bear right onto Pozo Road and drive 15 miles to Pozo. Continue another mile on Pozo Road.to a "T" intersection. Pozo Road turns right here. We continue straight 3 miles on the San Jose-La Panza Road to the El Pozo Grade Road. Turn right onto this road toward Turkey Flats. Follow this narrow, winding, but paved road 3 miles to a saddle looking down on Highway 58. There are three roads here. The right heads to Navajo Camp, while the middle road takes you down to Friis Camp, cutting 2 miles off your journey. The left road heads to the FAA Radar Station and our trailhead 2.3 miles up the paved road. A sign "Friis Camp" marks the trailhead itself. It is located on a right turn and may be hard to see. There is parking for about six cars on the left.

To shuttle this trip, return 2.3 miles to the El Pozo Grade Road. Take the second road to the left (not the road to Friis Camp) and go downhill past Navajo Camp. After 1.1 mile bear left across the creek and go up a small steep rise on Mc Ginnis Creek Road. Drive 2 miles to the junction of

Fernandez and Red Hill Road. Turn left on Fernandez Road and drive 1.2 mile to the Red Wind Ranch gate and park your car on the side of the road. Shuttling this trip sometimes takes longer than retracing your steps.

Trail Overview: The Fernandez Trail is one of the best-kept secrets in the La Panza Range. The trail starts at an elevation 2900' and meanders down through a series of scenic side canyons off the eastern crest of the La Panza Range. It continues to Fernandez Road near the Bethel Ranch at elevation 1700'. In fall, the area's varied vegetation produces fascinating contrasts of colors and textures of golden grasses, cottonwoods, pink buckwheat, whitish manzanita on red trunks and dark green live oaks and grey pines. In spring the green meadows on each side of the trail abound with wildflowers such as shooting stars, wild peony, yellow violets, popcorn flower, baby blue eyes, miners lettuce, yucca and Sierra currant.

This trail was adopted by the Central Coast Concerned Mountain Bikers (CCCMB), who continue to maintain it.

Trail Description:

Fernandez Trailhead. Our trail starts east with a gradual descent on the south side of the canyon, with Fernandez Creek below. We wind in and out of these canyons as we head toward Friis Camp. On these slopes you find the earliest of the spring wildflowers, including shooting stars and peony. The trail ducks behind a small knoll, then reappears above Fernandez Creek with a small outcropping to the left. During the winter months a small but impressive

Waterfall is a pleasant surprise. A side trail takes us to the top of the fall. Leaving the waterfall behind we are much closer to Fernandez Creek. Accompanied by the sound of running water, we follow the creek 0.3 mile to reach

Friis Camp. At Friis Camp you find the alternate access to the Fernandez Trail. There is a water tank and a stock pond. This trough provides drinking water for the wild horses and other animals of the area. The trail leaves Friis Camp on the north side to follow Fernandez Creek. It crosses the creek several times, eventually coming to a tributary entering from the east. Here is the junction to Friis Public Camp, where three areas are available for overnight camping. Jumping the tributary, we follow Fernandez Creek's east bank for the next 0.5 mile. Enjoy the wide variety of oaks, grey pines and a host of wildflowers. We climb over a rocky outcropping, then descend to a

meadow. The meadow makes a great lunch spot, and gives us the opportunity to explore Fernandez Creek. Our trail leaves the creek, turning to the east. If you wish to make a semi-loop, continue to follow Fernandez Creek 2.2 miles to Fernandez Road, turn right on Fernandez Road, follow it about 0.5 mile to another road junction, and turn right again to return to the Fernandez Trail. This route is only for the experienced hiker: it is very rocky, heavily vegetated, and at times full of poison oak. Staying on the main trail, we head east climbing through a side canyon to a

crest overlooking the valley ahead. The Central Coast Concerned Mountain Bikers (CCCMB) installed a wooden bench here. There are a few tools under the bench for those inclined to do trail work. Be sure to return them to their storage area. We now make a short but steep descent to a small creek. We cross the creek to reach a rocky outcropping. If there is water in the creek, a small waterfall can be seen tumbling over the rocks. From here we continue our rolling descent over small hills. The trail then reaches the creek and follows it 0.2 mile to

Fernandez Road. A motor vehicle stop marks the beginning of the trails. This is where our alternate cross-country route will rejoin the Fernandez Trail. The road is closed at times, making it necessary to follow Fernandez Road to the locked gate. To follow the road, turn right and travel 1.5 mile to the locked gate and the

end of the FernandezTrail.

MORRO BAY
SAND SPIT

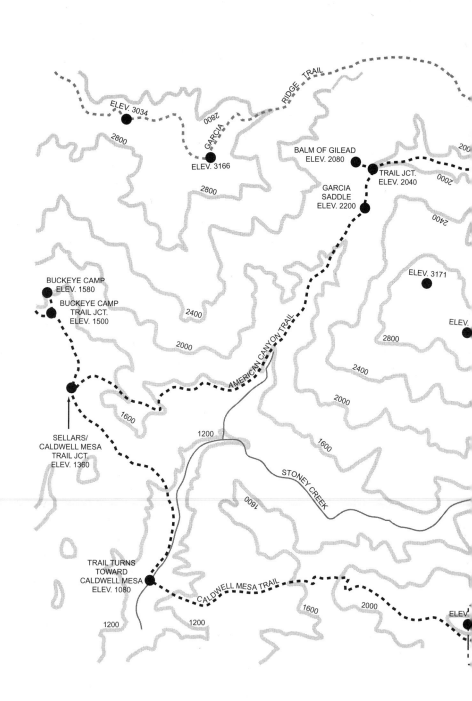

American Canyon

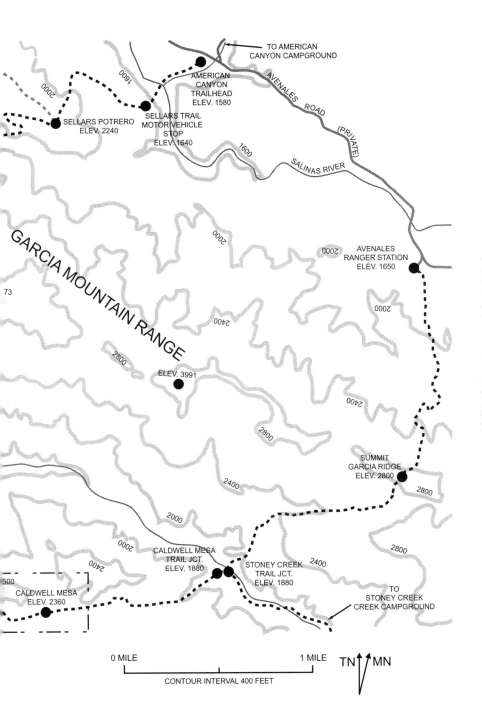

TO AMERICAN
CANYON CAMPGROUND

AMERICAN
CANYON
TRAILHEAD
ELEV. 1580

AVENALES   ROAD   (PRIVATE)

SELLARS POTRERO
ELEV. 2240

SELLARS TRAIL
MOTOR VEHICLE
STOP
ELEV. 1640

SALINAS RIVER

GARCIA MOUNTAIN RANGE

73

AVENALES
RANGER STATION
ELEV. 1650

ELEV. 3991

SUMMIT
GARCIA RIDGE
ELEV. 2800

CALDWELL MESA
TRAIL JCT.
ELEV. 1880

STONEY CREEK
TRAIL JCT.
ELEV. 1880

TO
STONEY CREEK
CREEK CAMPGROUND

500

CALDWELL MESA
ELEV. 2360

0 MILE   1 MILE

TN   MN

CONTOUR INTERVAL 400 FEET

177

American Canyon to Buckeye Camp

Usage:	Hikers, Horses and Dogs
Fee:	None, but Permission Required (See Below).
Distance:	6.5 Miles One Way
Elevation Gain/Loss:	+1000/ -1200 Feet
Approx. Hiking Time:	8 - 10 Hours
Hike Rating:	Strenuous
USGS Maps:	Pozo Summit, Caldwell Mesa

Best Time to Hike: Winter, Spring, Late Fall

Point On Route:	Distance from Starting Point Miles (Km)	Elevation
American Canyon /Avenales Road Trailhead	0.0 (0.0)	1580
Sellars Trail/Motor Vehicle Stop	0.4 (0.6)	1640
Sellars Potrero/Gate	1.6 (2.6)	2240
Balm Gilead Trail Junction	2.8 (4.5)	2040
Garcia Saddle	3.0 (4.8)	2200
Sellars/Caldwell Mesa Trail Junction	5.9 (9.5)	1360
Junction to Buckeye Camp	6.4 (10.3)	1500
Buckeye Camp	6.5 (10.5)	1600

Directions to Trailhead: Take the Santa Margarita (Hwy. 58) exit from US 101 and turn east toward Santa Margarita. Turn right on Hwy 58. At the junction with Pozo Road and Hwy. 58, follow the signs to Santa Margarita Lake (Pozo Road). Drive approximately 7 miles to the Santa Margarita Lake turnoff. Continue straight 11 miles to Pozo. Continue straight 1.4 miles to the intersection of Park Hill and Pozo Roads and turn right onto Pozo Road. Drive 1.5 miles to another intersection with Avenales Road. Continue straight on Avenales Road 3.5 miles to a locked gate. *This gate is only open during deer hunting season (mid-August to late September).* At any other time, contact the US Forest Service for a permit. Assuming you have your permit, continue 1.9 miles along this road to the American Canyon Road junction. Park here and leave a note on your car.

Trail Overview: This wonderful hike explores the Garcia Mountain range. It climbs the front range to Sellars Potrero (Potrero means "horse pasture" in Spanish), then descends into an oak-studded valley before reaching Balm of Gilead. The trail then climbs to a saddle of the Garcia ridge before descending through an oak forest along a creek. There is another short climb before our final descent to Stoney Creek. Once at Stoney Creek, we head upstream to Buckeye Camp, a delightful spot under huge oaks and bay trees.

A shuttle trip, 11 miles one way, can be made to Pozo-Arroyo Grande Road. See Trout Creek Trail description for details.

Trail Description:

American Canyon Road Junction Trailhead. Our trail begins immediately south of the junction. Look for an old road, intermittently marked by posts, through an open field. Head south to the Salinas River and follow it into an oak and pine forest. The old road now crosses the

Salinas River, a wet crossing in rainy season. Go past the motor vehicle stop directly across the river and look for a trail to the right. This is the easier trail to Sellars Potrero. Take the right fork and head into the forest. The trail wanders through the forest and climbs slowly to the ridge above Avenales Road. We now head south and ascend the ridge to

Sellars Potrero. Be sure to close the gate after passing through. Our route continues west along the hillside. You may notice a fork to the right that appears to rise to the ridge. This trail will take you to Garcia Mountain along an old fire road and motorcycle route. We continue level through meadows with an occasional tree. The trail then makes a sharp left to descend several switchbacks to the valley below. The trail may appear to follow the creek downstream, but it really heads upstream across the meadow into an oak forest. From here to the junction of Balm of Gilead, beware of poison oak along the trail. The valley of oaks is quite pleasant as we travel 0.5 mile to the

Balm of Gilead Campground Junction. The campground is a short 0.1 mile beyond this junction. At the campground there is a fire pit, an open area for a tent, and a dilapidated picnic table. From this junction we now turn left to ascend Garcia Ridge to

Garcia Saddle which leads us down to Stoney Creek and Caldwell Mesa. The terrain alternates between chaparral and oak woodland. We soon come to a small creek, which appears to run year-round. The trail crosses the creek several times. Surprisingly, lush ferns and horsetails can be found in many spots along the stream. After following the creek for a little more than a mile, the trail makes one more crossing, switches back, and makes a short ascent, leaving the stream for good. The trail then rises onto a hot sunny slope of thick chaparral 200 – 300 feet above the stream. Eventually the trail starts to level off, skirting the hillside toward a nearby ridge. The trail crosses this ridge, then starts a switchbacked descent, becoming less obvious just before Stoney Creek. Cross the creek to the

Caldwell Mesa/Buckeye Camp Trail Junction. If you want to reach Caldwell Mesa, turn left here. Otherwise, turn right and head upstream toward Buckeye Camp. The old Forest Service sign can be found on the ground 100 yards past the junction. This is one of the few remaining signs in the Garcia Wilderness Area—please do not remove. We continue along Stoney Creek and reach the

Buckeye Camp Trail Junction. Turn right here and walk 0.1 mile to

Buckeye Camp. Buckeye trees are nowhere to be seen, but the camp is densely shaded by large oak and bay trees. It makes a good lunch spot and a place to cool off. At the camp there is a fire pit and running water from a spring. There may be a wilderness toilet nearby as well.

If you are making a shuttle trip, return to the Buckeye Camp Trail Junction and take the right fork to the Pozo-Arroyo Grande Road. Otherwise retrace your steps to American Canyon.

CASTLE CRAGS,
MACHESNA
WILDERNESS

M.FOSTER

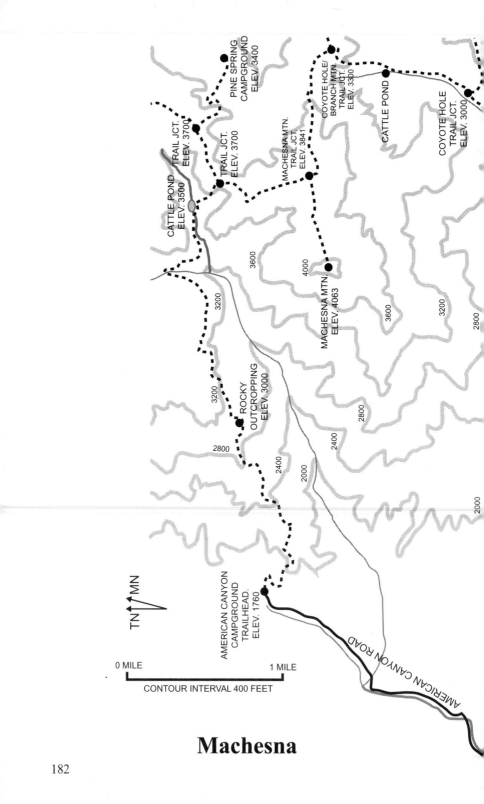

PINE SPRING
CAMPGROUND
ELEV. 3400

COYOTE HOLE/
BRANCH MTN.
TRAIL JCT.
ELEV. 3300

TRAIL JCT.
ELEV. 3700

TRAIL JCT.
ELEV. 3700

CATTLE POND

MACHESNA MTN.
TRAIL JCT.
ELEV. 3841

COYOTE HOLE
TRAIL JCT.
ELEV. 3000

CATTLE POND
ELEV. 3500

3600

4000

3600

3200

2800

MACHESNA MTN.
ELEV. 4063

3200

ROCKY
OUTCROPPING
ELEV. 3000

2800

2800

2400

2000

2400

2000

2000

AMERICAN CANYON
CAMPGROUND
TRAILHEAD.
ELEV. 1760

AMERICAN CANYON ROAD

TN MN

0 MILE   1 MILE

CONTOUR INTERVAL 400 FEET

Machesna

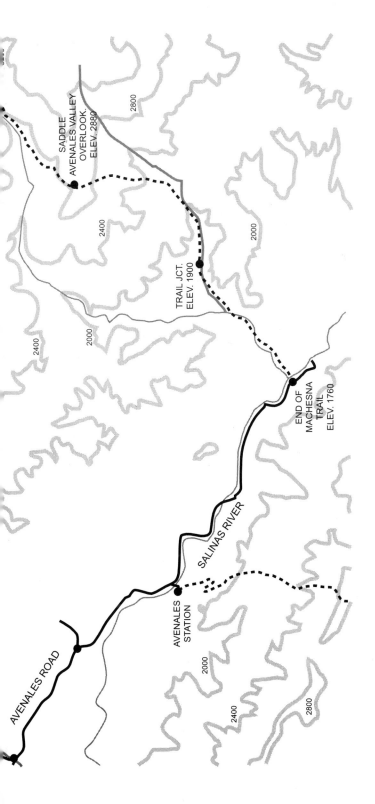

SADDLE
AVENALES VALLEY
OVERLOOK.
ELEV. 2880

2800

2400

2000

2400

2000

TRAIL JCT.
ELEV. 1900

END OF
MACHESNA
TRAIL
ELEV. 1760

SALINAS RIVER

AVENALES
STATION

2000

2400

2800

AVENALES ROAD

183

Machesna Mountain

Usage:	Hikers and Horses
Fee:	None at press time, but permission to pass may be required.
Distance:	10.5-Mile Shuttle (11.8 with Side Trip)
Elevation Gain/Loss:	+3000/-3000 Feet
Approx. Hiking Time:	8 - 10 Hours
Hike Rating:	Strenuous
USGS Maps:	La Panza, Los Machos Hills

Best Time to Hike: Winter, Spring, Late Fall

Point On Route:	Distance from Starting Point Miles(Km)	Elevation
American Canyon Campground Trailhead	0.0 (0.0)	1750
Rocky Outcropping	2.0 (3.2)	3200
Creek Crossing	3.4 (5.5)	3300
Gate at Cattle Pond	4.0 (6.4)	3500
Cattle Pond	4.1 (6.6)	3500
Machesna/Pine Springs Camp Trail Junction	4.3 (6.9)	3740
Machesna Mountain Trail Junction	5.1 (8.2)	3840
Coyote Hole/Branch Mtn. Trail Junction	6.0 (9.7)	3360
Cattle Pond/Creek Crossing	6.5 (10.5)	3000
Coyote Hole Fork Trail Junction	7.0 (11.3)	3000
Avenales Valley Overlook	8.1 (13.0)	2880
Base of hill	8.9 (14.3)	2000
Avenales Road	10.5 (16.9)	1800

Directions to Trailhead: Take the Santa Margarita (Hwy. 58) exit from US 101. Turn east toward Santa Margarita and turn right on Hwy. 58. At the junction with Pozo Road and Hwy. 58, follow the signs to Santa Margarita Lake (Pozo Road). Drive approximately 7 miles to the Santa Margarita Lake turnoff. Continue straight on Pozo Road for another 11 miles until you reach Pozo. Continue straight 1.4 mile to the intersection of Park Hill and Pozo Road. Turn right onto Pozo Road. Drive 1.5 mile to another intersection with the Avenales Road. Continue straight on the Avenales Road 3.5 miles to a locked gate. *This gate is only open during hunting season (mid-August to late September).* At any other time, contact the US Forest Service for permission to enter. Assuming you have your permit, continue 1.9 mile along this road to the American Canyon Road junction.

For a shuttle trip, drive another 3.6 miles along the Avenales Road to place your car at the other end of the trail. This spot is not marked and is easy to miss. If you encounter a sharp left turn followed by a sharp right turn, you have gone about 0.1 mile too far. Return to the American Canyon Junction to drive 1.2 miles to the campground. Be sure to close all gates after passing.

Trail Overview: This is a loop trail (including shuttle) encompassing 4063' Machesna Mountain. It is mainly in the Machesna Wilderness, though it begins and ends on private property. In the first 4 miles the trail ascends 1700' to join the trail from Queen Bee Campground. It then climbs through chaparral to the intersection due east of Machesna Mountain, where a detour can be made to the summit. The trail then traverses a ridge and descends into Coyote Hole before climbing the last ridge and descending to Avenales Road. Wildflowers make a splendid show in late winter and early spring.

Trail Description:

    American Canyon Trailhead. The trail begins at the north end of oak-covered American Canyon Campground. Pit toilets are available. Please sign in. Take the trail up the hill to the right. We quickly climb above the campground for a view of the valley below. At 0.6 mile the trail leaves the oak-covered meadow and enters an area mainly covered by chamise. The trail steepens quickly as it winds up the open slopes. At the 2-mile point the trail starts to level out and reaches a

    Rocky outcropping which makes an excellent rest stop. From here the trail enters what used to be a pine forest currently recovering from the Highway 58 fire of 1997. The grade then lessens and the hike becomes much more enjoyable. The trail dips in and out of two canyons, descending 100 feet on the second one. It reaches a

    small creek, then quickly climbs for another view of Machesna Mountain. The trail now starts to round a bend with a rocky creek below, and Machesna Mountain across the valley. Following the creek we reach a

    gate just before the cattle pond, which should remain closed. Immediately after the gate, the trail crosses over a dam of the

    cattle pond to a large meadow filled with shooting stars, popcorn and other flowers during the spring months. This makes an excellent lunch stop after your long climb. You may see a few frogs in the pond. Leaving the cattle pond the trail heads southeast up the valley to the

Pine Springs Trail Junction, then continues up to the ridge. From the ridge we can see the Temblor Range, Caliente Mountain and Carrisa Plain. The trail, now an old fire road, passes through a gate that climbs steeply through open chaparral before leveling out to reach the

Machesna Mountain Trail Junction. To climb Machesna Mountain, take the right trail for a 1.3 mile round trip detour. Since the Highway 58 fire the views from the top are less obstructed. If you have chosen not to climb Machesna, continue straight 200 yards to a meadow for a leisurely stop. Our trail continues straight, then swings left along a fire road as it descends to the

CoyoteHole/Branch Mountain Trail Junction. Take the right fork and follow the old road while descending into Coyote Hole. There will be a

cattle pond on your right. Cross the small creek and follow the nearly level trail along the creek for about 0.5 mile. Here we reach the

Coyote Hole Fork. It appears the trail might continue along the ranch road, then climb out of the valley. *Do not take it—this is the wrong route.* Follow the much more obscure cattle trail which skirts the contours of the creek and a fence. The trail then widens up 200 yards ahead. We now enter thick brush as we descend 400' on a steep rocky slope. We continue along the creek a short distance, then start a climb over oak-covered grasslands to a wire gate. Pass through the gate and enjoy the view from the

saddle overlooking Avenales Valley. From here we start a steep 900' drop along a rocky trail to the valley below. Once at the

base of the hill, continue following the creek downstream along old cattle trails reaching the old road and a small concrete bridge. The trail leaves the road immediately past the bridge and continues to follow the creek downstream. Crossing the creek a few times, we come to a place where water has eroded a cliff, creating a wonderful sandstone formation. We continue downstream where two creeks join. Cross the creek here. Keep heading south along the stream, crossing it several times. Staying on the left side of the stream, we finally see our destination,

Avenales Road. Cross the stream to return to your car.

Margaret Foster

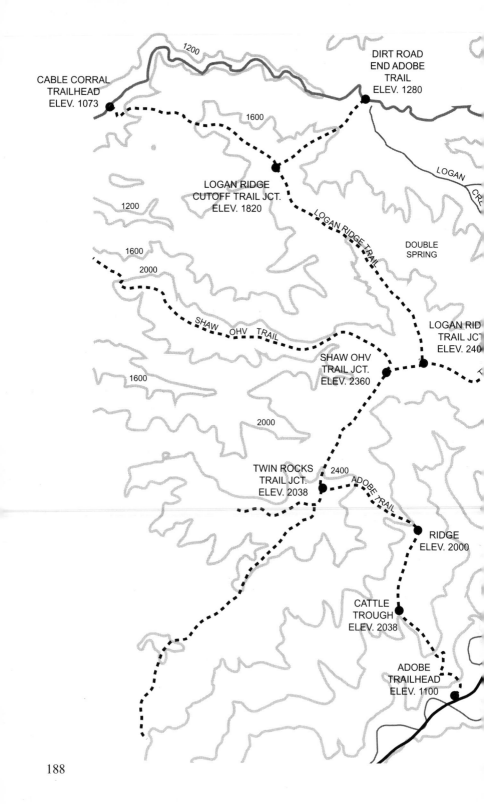

CABLE CORRAL
TRAILHEAD
ELEV. 1073

1200

DIRT ROAD
END ADOBE
TRAIL
ELEV. 1280

1600

LOGAN

CR

LOGAN RIDGE
CUTOFF TRAIL JCT.
ELEV. 1820

LOGAN RIDGE TRAIL

DOUBLE
SPRING

1200

1600

2000

SHAW OHV TRAIL

LOGAN RID
TRAIL JCT
ELEV. 240

1600

SHAW OHV
TRAIL JCT.
ELEV. 2360

2000

TWIN ROCKS
TRAIL JCT.
ELEV. 2038

2400

ADOBE TRAIL

RIDGE
ELEV. 2000

CATTLE
TROUGH
ELEV. 2038

ADOBE
TRAILHEAD
ELEV. 1100

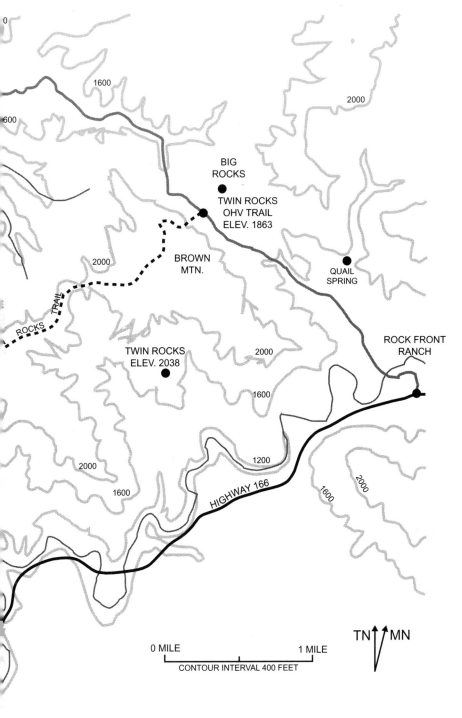

0

1600

2000

600

BIG
ROCKS

●

TWIN ROCKS
OHV TRAIL
ELEV. 1863

●

2000

BROWN
MTN.

QUAIL
SPRING

●

ROCKS TRAIL

ROCK FRONT
RANCH

TWIN ROCKS
ELEV. 2038

●

2000

1600

●

1200

2000

HIGHWAY 166

1600

1600

2000

1600

0 MILE   1 MILE

TN ↑↑ MN

CONTOUR INTERVAL 400 FEET

Adobe

Adobe

Usage:	Hikers, Horses, Mountain Bikes, and Dogs
Fee:	Adventure Pass
Distance:	6.5 Miles (One Way)
Elevation Gain/Loss:	+1530/-1350
Approx. Hiking Time:	3-5 Hours
Hike Rating:	Moderately Strenuous
USGS Maps:	Chimney Canyon, Los Machos Hills

Best Time to Hike: Winter, Spring, Late Fall

Point On Route:	Distance from Starting Point Miles(Km)	Elevation
Adobe Trailhead	0.0 (0.0)	1100
Cattle Trough	1.3 (2.1)	1600
Ridge	1.8 (2.9)	2000
Twin Rocks Trail	2.6 (4.2)	2470
Unknown Trail Junction	3.1 (5.0)	2240
Shaw OHV Trail	3.7 (6.0)	2360
Logan Ridge Trail	3.9 (6.2)	2400
Faint Trail	5.7 (9.1)	1820
Dirt road	6.5 (10.4)	1280

Directions to Trailhead: Take U.S. 101 to Highway 166, just north of the Santa Maria River. Turn east and drive 22 miles, which will take you past Twitchell Reservoir and cross the Cuyama River several times. Watch for a sign reading "Adobe Trail, Branch Creek, Thirty Five Canyon" on the left-hand side of the road. It should be located between two bridges over Cuyama River on Highway 166. If you reach Rock Front Ranch, you have driven too far by 3.8 miles. The trailhead resembles a small corral with space for about 20 cars. Drive into the parking area and close the gate if you found it closed. The first part of the trail, to the ridge, is not shown on current USGS Topo maps.

Shuttle Directions: Three shuttle trips are possible:

Big Rocks Shuttle: Drive east on Highway 166 3.8 miles to the Rock Front Ranch. Turn left onto the Forest Service road and cross the Cuyama River over a concrete culvert. Follow the road 2.3 miles to the intersection of the Twin Rocks Trail.

Cattle Ramp Shuttle: Continue past Big Rocks, down a steep and winding road, 2.2 miles to a cattle loading ramp. A four-wheel drive vehicle may be needed to reach this spot.

Cable Corral Spring: Drive another 2.5 miles on the dirt road to Cable Corral Spring, elevation 1078. A four-wheel drive vehicle may be needed.

Trail Overview: The Adobe Trail is a patchwork of foot and jeep trails over two ridges covered by chaparral and oak-studded grassland. It is located in the Twin Rocks area of the Los Padres National Forest. After climbing a steep hillside, the trail dips into a canyon with a spring, then emerges to climb a ridge and join the Twin Rocks Trail. It then descends and climbs a second ridge before dropping along Logan Ridge to Branch Creek. In late winter and spring abundant wildflowers are found along the trail, including penstemon, mariposa lilies, goldfields and tidy tips.

Many trips are possible in this area, all worth the effort. Bring plenty of water—it can be quite hot here in late spring and during the summer months. Gaiters are also recommended for late spring and summer trips because of the abundance of foxtails and spring grasses.

Trail Description:

Adobe Trailhead. The trail starts at the right rear of the parking area. Please close the gate after passing. The trail makes a quick but short climb to an open meadow, where it may be faint and sometimes overgrown with grass. Watch for the left-hand turn which starts a series of switchbacks up the hill, beginning with two long traverses. The old adobe homestead below, which gave this trail its name, is the Permasse Ranch. The trail reaches the top of the first point, then heads into a canyon for a couple of last switchbacks before it rounds a second point and heads into a narrow canyon. We then enter chaparral and chamise as we descend 100 feet to a seasonal creek. 100 yards ahead we reach the

old cattle trough which is still in use today. The large oaks in this site make it a good place to cool off on a warm day. Leaving the cattle trough behind, the trail follows the creek through willows, oaks and occasional poison oak, crossing it several times before climbing to a

ridge. Once on the ridge, turn left to follow the trail straight up the ridgeline, quite steeply in places. Be sure to stay on the ridgeline, as the trail may be overgrown with spring grass. Flowers are abundant here in spring. Once on top we find an old jeep trail called the

"Twin Rocks Trail" at elevation 2470 feet. The hiker may want to explore the open meadow surrounded by oak trees. It makes a good lunch spot and a good turnaround place if you are not doing a shuttle. If you are continuing, take the road to the right, north, following the Twin Rocks Trail. The trail descends slightly, traversing the ridge. A half-mile ahead we come to an unknown

trail junction. Take the right fork. The left fork has not been explored at this time. The trail descends to a picturesque valley and reaches a

locked gate. Pass through or climb over the gate on the hinge side, and ascend the trail ridge in front of you. Reaching the crest of the ridge, we come to the Shaw Canyon OHV Trail to the left. Continue straight for another 0.2 mile to reach the Logan Ridge Trail. Depending on where you have left your car, you may continue straight, following the Twin Rocks Trail line to Brown Mountain and Big Rocks. This is the preferred route during wet weather. Our route turns left down Logan Ridge. Logan Ridge is well known for the many wildflowers located here. Large fields of blooming flowers in the spring make the hills alive with color. Once on Logan Ridge the route is all downhill. Approximately 1.7 miles down the ridge, look for a

faint trail junction to the right following the ridgeline. Turn right onto this trail, then travel another 0.8 mile to the dirt road, our ending point. If you miss this junction, you will need to walk 1.5 miles to Cable Corral Spring. Once at the dirt road, turn right and walk the 2.5 miles back to the trail end.

Unexplored Los Padres National Forest

Los Padres National Forest is crisscrossed with trails, and many could not be documented. In order not to lose sight of these areas, and to keep the public informed to the best of our knowledge, we have included five in this section. Some have been traveled prior to being included in this guide, some have not. Before venturing in, we recommend that you inform yourself thoroughly on access points and current road and trail conditions. For information, contact the government agency that has jurisdiction over the area, usually the local U. S. Forest Service Office.

Caldwell Mesa to Buckeye Camp

Usage:	Hikers, Horses and Dogs
Fee:	Adventure Pass
Distance:	7.0 Miles (One Way)
Elevation Gain/Loss:	+1500/-1600 Feet
Approx. Hiking Time:	4-6 Hours
Hike Rating:	Moderately Strenuous
USGS Maps:	Caldwell Mesa, Pozo Summit

Best Time to Hike: Winter, Spring and Late Fall

The Caldwell Mesa Trail follows the Stony (also spelled "Stoney") Creek Trail for two miles, then heads left along a creek to reach Caldwell Mesa. After crossing this beautiful mesa, it passes Bonnet Rock before descending to Stony Creek. Once on the creek, we head upstream through lush vegetation, intersect the American Canyon trail, and finally reach Buckeye Camp.

Unfortunately, access to this trail has become increasingly difficult in recent years due to overuse, excessive parties, property damage, and property line disputes. The access road has been closed near Agua Escondido Camp, also closed, approximately five miles from the Stony Creek Trailhead.

Directions to Trailhead: From Arroyo Grande follow Grand Avenue east towards Lopez Lake. Approximately two miles from Arroyo Grande, turn right onto Huasna Road (Lopez Drive goes straight). Drive 1.6 miles, crossing Branch Mill Road, to another intersection. Bear to the right, staying on Huasna Road. Eight miles further there will be another intersection. Continue straight, drive up over the hill and descend to a large wooden bridge over Huasna River. The road turns to dirt and we come to an intersection with a sign pointing the way to Stony Creek and Agua Escondido Campgrounds. The gate may be occasionally closed and locked. In any case, leave the gate as you found it when passing through.

For the next nine miles you will be driving on private property. Please respect the rights of the property owner by staying on the road rather than venturing into the surrounding area. After several creek crossings we come to an intersection. The right fork has a locked gate to Jolon Ranch. Take the left fork to ascend the ridge and enter the Los Padres National Forest. Drive to where the road is blocked and park your car off the road near Agua Escondido Campground. From here it is another 5 miles along a dirt road to Stony Creek Campground. You will have to ride your mountain bike, horse, or walk this distance on foot. If you ride your mountain bike to reach the

Stony Creek Campground Trailhead, you will have to leave it at the campground when continuing onto Caldwell Mesa. Bikes are not allowed in the Garcia Wilderness, which starts just past the trailhead.

Trail Description:

Stony Creek Campground Trailhead. Leave the campground and follow the road to the left, downhill, into the Garcia Wilderness. Pine Ridge is ahead to the left, covered with Coulter Pines. After ½ mile along the road we come to the first of three creek crossings, this one on an old stone bridge built years ago for cattle and wagons. The second creek crossing, with huge granite boulders ahead on the left, is at 1.3 miles. At 1.6 miles, we cross the creek a third time. Follow the road for another 0.4 mile. At this point the road ends. Look for signs of a faint trail on the right hand side. Alternately, look for the Caldwell Mesa trail on the left. If you can find either one, you are in the right place, as they are across from each other. The Caldwell Mesa Trail is easier to find than the Stony Creek trail, because it is marked by a ridge on the right and a creek flowing just to the side. These trails may be marked now with official signs.

From here we leave the roadway, starting a gentle 0.8-mile climb along the creek to reach an open plateau, Caldwell Mesa, a private inholding in Los Padres National Forest. The large open meadow with mature oaks makes a great place for a picnic. The trail heads west across the meadow towards a knoll, elevation 2500 feet. A large cattle pond is on our left. Reaching the other side of the meadow, the trail enters thick chaparral, starting a two-mile descent along the ridge to Bonnet Rock and ending at Stony Creek. Here the trail turns to the right following Stony Creek up stream 1.4 miles, intersecting the trail from American Canyon. From here, walk another half mile upstream to Buckeye Camp.

Caliente Mountain

Usage:	Hikers, Horses, and Dogs
Fee:	None at this Time
Distance:	8.0 or 14.5 Miles (One Way)
Elevation Gain/Loss:	+3420 Feet
Approx. Hiking Time:	6-8 Hours
Hike Rating:	Strenuous
USGS Maps:	Taylor Canyon, Caliente Mountain

Best Time to Hike: Winter and Spring

Caliente Mountain, at elevation 5106, is the highest mountain in San Luis Obispo County. The first 2.4 miles of trail from Highway 166 run across an easement through private lands. This easement was secured in the spring of 1987 through the efforts of several organizations: the Bureau of Land Management (BLM), Sportsmen's Council, Wildlife Conservation Board, Civilian Conservation Corps (CCC), and the Sierra Club, as well as several individuals. Please respect the right of the owner by staying on the easement. Wildflowers thrive here in spring, but in the dry season this is a very hot and dusty trail. Be sure to carry in plenty of water.

Directions to Trailhead:

Highway 166 Access: Take U.S. 101 to Highway 166, just north of the Santa Maria River. Head east on 166 and drive 38.1 miles, past Twitchell Reservoir, Rock Front Ranch at 25 miles, and Spanish Ranch at 34 miles. Watch for a gate on the left. There is a small turnout parking area just east of the trailhead. From this trailhead, 14.5 miles and a 3240-foot climb take the hiker to the top of Caliente Mountain.

California Valley Access: From San Luis Obispo, take US 101 north and Highway 58 east to California Valley. Turn right on Soda Lake Road and look for a sign indicating "Guy L. Goodwin Education Center." Just past this sign is a dirt road to Selby Rocks. Turn right here and follow the signs to the Caliente Mountain Trailhead on the west side of the mountain. This road is impassable in wet weather, and may require four-wheel drive in spring and summer as well. From this trailhead, the distance to the top of Caliente Mountain is eight miles, elevation gain 1200 feet.

Trail Description:

Caliente Mountain Trailhead. At the trailhead is a sign, "Access Route to Caliente Resources Lands," followed by a sign dedicating the trail. The trail follows a set of markers as it crosses private land. At 1.1 miles the trail crosses a saddle, then descends through a juniper grove and turns to the left. At the 1.6 mile point the trail turns right, northerly. We come to a metal gate, the old Rancho Cuyama line. The trail eventually descends into a dry creek bed through a juniper grove, then reaches a vicinity map showing the trail location and route ahead. We are now on public lands. The trail crosses a mesa, then starts a slow ascent up the ridge.

At the 3.3-mile point we come to a fork in the trail. Bear right here and climb to the ridgeline. An old oil site can be seen at the ridgeline, and power lines to the northeast. According to the book, we now head cross-country toward the power lines for the next 1.2 miles, climbing 900 feet to elevation 3720'. At this point we come to an old roadway, a well traveled jeep trail. Follow the roadway around Morales Canyon along the ridge. There are spectacular views of Mount Able, Cuyama Valley, Sierras, and Caliente Mountain. Follow the roadway uphill towards the radio tower.

At 4.9 miles a fork in the road is reached. The elevation here is 3800 feet. Bear right towards the radio tower, then pass it 0.4 mile ahead. At 5.5 miles, bear right again at the fork to pass the second radio tower. Continue 0.9 mile ahead to reach a fork in the jeep road, elevation 3950 feet. This is the

California Valley Trailhead, elevation 4090'. From here it is 8 miles to the top of Caliente Mountain. We follow the jeep road east to pass an old oil well site on the left. From this point on to the top, no real trail description exists. Follow the ridge line along the road and/or trail to the top of Caliente Peak at elevation 5106 feet.

Gifford Ranch

Usage:	Hikers, Horses and Dogs
Fee:	Adventure Pass
Distance:	Uknown, at Least 2 Miles (One Way)
Elevation Gain/Loss:	Unknown
Approx. Hiking Time:	3-5 Hours
Hike Rating:	Moderately Strenuous
USGS Maps:	Branch Mountain, Miranda Pine Mountain

Best Time to Hike: Winter, Spring, Late Fall

Directions to Trailhead: Take Highway 101 to Highway 166, just north of the Santa Maria River. Drive 27.1 miles east on 166, past Twitchell Reservoir and past Rock Front Ranch at 25 miles. 2.1 miles after passing Rock Front Ranch, look for a small pullout on the left-hand side of the road. Drive through the wire gate and close it behind you. Park in any open area you wish. The trail is located on the northwest side of the parking area.

Trail Overview: The Gifford Ranch Trail is mainly used by horses, but it does explore the area southeast of Branch Mountain and a part of Gifford Ranch itself. Initially, the trail heads up a small ridge towards power lines, then crosses through an open meadow to descend to Gypsum Canyon. From here the trail turns north, but we are unsure of its destination or exact route. If you know more about this route and its actual destination please write to the Sierra Club at *P.O. 15755, San Luis Obispo, CA 93406, attn: Trail Guide Update*, or via E-mail through our website at *www.sierraclub.org/chapters/santalucia.*

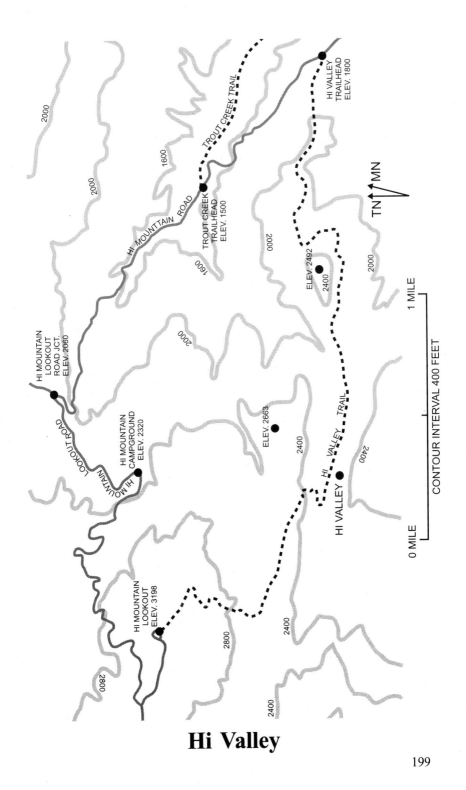

Hi Valley

199

Hi Valley

Usage:	Hikers, Horses and Dogs
Fee:	None at this Time
Distance:	4.2 Miles (One Way)
Elevation Gain/Loss:	+2000/-200
Approx. Hiking Time:	2-4 Hours
Hike Rating:	Moderately Strenuous
USGS Maps:	Santa Margarita Lake, Tar Spring Ridge

Best Time to Hike: Winter and Spring

The Hi Valley Trail was once closed to protect the peregrine falcons that
have nested in the area. The trail is now open for use by hikers and horses.
We are unsure about mountain bikes. The trail itself explores the western
side of Hi Mountain Road with a walk through Hi Valley and a climb of 2000
feet to Hi Mountain Lookout itself. The lookout is currently being restored
to be used for bird watching.

Directions to Trailhead: Take the Santa Margarita (Hwy. 58) exit from US
101. Turn east toward Santa Margarita and turn right on Hwy. 58. At the
junction with Pozo Road and Hwy. 58, follow the signs to Santa Margarita
Lake (Pozo Road). Drive approximately 7 miles to the Santa Margarita Lake
turnoff. Continue straight on Pozo Road for another 11 miles until you reach
Pozo. Turn right onto Hi Mountain Road, in front of the Ranger Station.
Drive one mile to the Salinas River. Cross the river and ascend the road for 4
miles to junction of Hi Mountain and Hi Mountain Lookout Road. Continue
straight down the hill approximately two miles, crossing two small streams
and the Trout Creek trailhead. From here drive 0.8 mile to the top of the ridge
to reach the Hi Valley Trailhead. This is marked by a pipe fence and trailhead
sign. This road is impassable in wet weather. It also may require four-wheel
drive at times.

Stony Creek

Usage:	Hikers, Horses and Dogs
Fee:	Adventure Pass
Distance:	5.5 Miles (One Way)
Elevation Gain/Loss:	+1000/-1500 Feet
Approx. Hiking Time:	4-6 Hours
Hike Rating:	Moderately Strenuous
USGS Maps:	Caldwell Mesa, Pozo Summit

Best Time to Hike: Winter, Spring and Late Fall

The Stony Creek Trail to Avenales Ranger Station rises steeply on the southwest side of Garcia Mountain. It ascends ridges with impressive views of Lopez Canyon to the west and the La Panza Range and Cuyama Valley to the southwest. Vegetation includes chaparral, oaks, bay trees and sycamores. The trail is marginally maintained and frequently overgrown. It is dry after Stony Creek, except for an isolated spring on the east flank of Garcia Mountain. This is reached by a side trail 1.5 miles from Avenales Station.

Unfortunately, access to this trail has become increasingly difficult in recent years due to overuse, excessive parties, property damage, and property line disputes. The access road has been closed near Agua Escondido Camp (also closed), approximately five miles from the Stony Creek Trailhead.

Directions to Trailhead: From Arroyo Grande follow Grand Avenue east towards Lopez Lake. Approximately two miles from Arroyo Grande, turn right onto Huasna Road (Lopez Drive goes straight). Drive 1.6 miles, crossing Branch Mill Road, to another intersection. Bear to the right, staying on Huasna Road. Eight miles further there will be another intersection. Continue straight, drive up over the hill and descend to a large wooden bridge over Huasna River. The road turns to dirt and we come to an intersection with a sign pointing the way to Stony Creek and Agua Escondido Campgrounds. The gate may be occasionally closed and locked. In any case, leave the gate as you found it when passing through.

For the next nine miles you will be driving on private property. Please respect the rights of the property owner by staying on the road rather than venturing into the surrounding area. After several creek crossings we come to an intersection. The right fork has a locked gate to Jolon Ranch. Take the left fork to ascend the ridge and enter the Los Padres National Forest. Drive to where the road is blocked and park your car off the road near Agua

Escondido Campground. From here it is another 5 miles along a dirt road to Stony Creek Campground. You will have to ride your mountain bike, horse, or walk this distance on foot. If you ride your bike you will have to leave it at Stony Creek Campground. Bikes are prohibited in the Garcia Wilderness, which starts just past the campground.

Trail Description:

Stony Creek Campground Trailhead. Leave the campground and follow the road to the left, downhill, into the Garcia Wilderness. Pine Ridge is ahead to the left, covered with Coulter Pines. After ½ mile along the road we come to the first of three creek crossings, this one on an old stone bridge built years ago for cattle and wagons. The second creek crossing, with huge granite boulders ahead on the left, is at 1.3 miles. At 1.6 miles, we cross the creek a third time. Follow the road for another 0.4 mile. At this point the road ends. Look for signs of a faint trail on the right hand side. Alternately, look for the Caldwell Mesa trail on the left. If you can find either one, you are in the right place, as they are across from each other. The Caldwell Mesa Trail is easier to find than the Stony Creek trail, because it is marked by a ridge on the right and a creek flowing just to the side. These trails may be marked now with official signs.

Assuming you have found the Stony Creek Trail on the right, the trail enters thick brush and chaparral. The trail climbs to the top of Garcia Mountain, elevation 2800 feet, 3.6 miles from Stony Creek Trailhead. It then descends steeply, dropping to 2350 feet in 0.4 mile, then makes a sharp right hand turn. In the remaining 1.5 miles the trail drops an additional 700 feet to reach the Avenales Ranger Station.

Lopez Lake

Tuouski – Two Waters
Hi Mountain

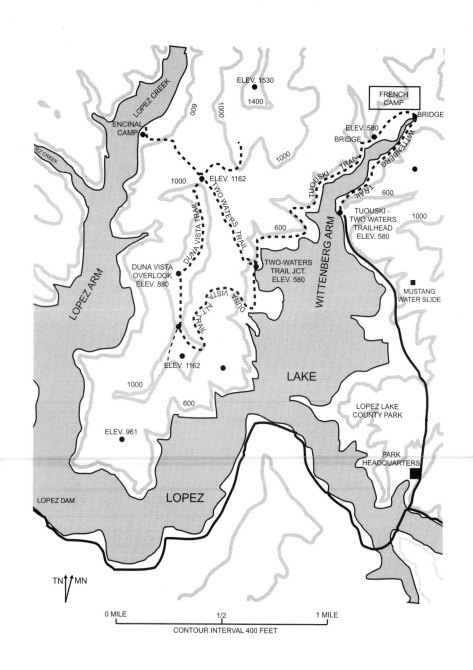

ELEV. 1530

FRENCH CAMP

BRIDGE

LOPEZ CREEK

ENCINAL CAMP

1400

ELEV. 580
BRIDGE

WITTENBERG TRAIL

TUOUSKI TRAIL

600

ELEV. 1162

TWO-WATERS TRAIL

1000

DUNA VISTA TRAIL

TUOUSKI - TWO WATERS TRAILHEAD
ELEV. 580

1000

600

600

LOPEZ ARM

DUNA VISTA OVERLOOK
ELEV. 880

WITTENBERG ARM

MUSTANG WATER SLIDE

DUNA VISTA ALT. TRAIL

TWO-WATERS TRAIL JCT.
ELEV. 580

ELEV. 1162

LAKE

LOPEZ LAKE COUNTY PARK

1000

600

ELEV. 961

PARK HEADQUARTERS

LOPEZ DAM

LOPEZ

TN ↑ MN

0 MILE   1/2   1 MILE

CONTOUR INTERVAL 400 FEET

Tuouski-Two Waters

204

Tuouski – Two Waters

Usage:	Only hikers and dogs on leash allowed beyond Tuouski Trailhead.
Fee:	Lopez Park Entrance Day Use Fee
Distance:	7.2 miles Round Trip (8.6 with Side Trip)
Elevation Gain/Loss:	+700/-700 Feet
Approx. Hiking Time:	4 Hours
Hike Rating:	Moderate
USGS Maps:	Lopez Lake

Best Time to Hike: Winter, Spring, Fall, Summer Evenings

Point On Route:	Distance from Starting Point Miles(Km)	Elevation
Lopez Lake	0.0 (0.0)	400
French Camp	0.8 (1.4)	440
Tuouski Trailhead	1.2 (1.9)	440
Two Waters Trail	2.4 (3.9)	400
Duna Vista Trail & Lopez Arm Junction	3.1 (5.0)	840
Duna Vista Overlook & Duna Vista Alt. Trail	3.6 (5.8)	1060
Cairns	3.9 (6.3)	1040
Two Waters Trail Junction	4.8 (7.7)	400
Tuouski Trailhead	6.0 (9.6)	440
French Camp Trailhead	6.3 (10.1)	440
Lopez Lake Trailhead	7.2 (11.5)	400

Directions to Trailhead: From San Luis Obispo, take Grand Ave. exit off Hwy 101 in Arroyo Grande and go left on Grand. After driving one mile east through Arroyo Grande Old Town, turn right on Lopez Drive and follow it to the Lopez Lake County Park Entrance, approximately 10 miles. Ask the ranger for a current area map. Ask for directions to the water slides and drive another 0.7 mile, past two gates, to the parking area just short of the Lopez Lake Trailhead. The trail starts 400 feet further down the road.

Trail Overview: This is a semi-loop trail that follows the Wittenberg Arm of Lopez Lake to French Camp, then continues on the other side of the Wittenberg Arm to the Tuouski, Two Waters and Duna Vista Trails. Our route takes us to an overlook with spectacular views of both arms of Lopez Lake, the surrounding hills, and the Oceano/Guadalupe Dunes in the distance. This trail offers a variety of terrains, including oak woodland, grassland and chaparral. Many examples of Monterey formations remind us that this area was once seabed. The climate here can vary greatly during the day and may be warmer than other areas along the coast. This is evident by the early bloom of spring wildflowers, appearing as early as January: milkmaids, miner's lettuce, poppies, hummingbird sage, blue dicks, ceanothus, johnny jump ups (yellow violets), red maids, baby blue eyes and an abundance of shooting stars. In addition to the many flowers, you may spot deer, white pelicans visiting for the winter, cormorants sitting in an old tree, and other bird species. Be prepared for poison oak and ticks—long pants are advisable. After a hot day's hike, it is possible to take a cooling dip in the lake.

Trail Description:

Lopez Lake Trailhead. The trail begins on a dirt road heading north towards French Camp. The hill to the right is carpeted with purple fiesta flowers in early spring. Along the road we twice pass the High Ridge Trail on the right. Continue on the road to a bridge crossing the Wittenberg Arm of Lopez Lake. We then come to

French Camp. From here the road crosses a small stream and follows the Eagle Scout row of pine trees on the left. At the end of this row the trail narrows as we reach the

Tuouski Trailhead. Mountain bikes and horses are forbidden from this point on. The shale formations at our feet are examples of the Monterey formations in the area. Taking a closer look, you may find fossil remains of clams and other shellfish. The trail winds in and out, up and down over several small hills, with the lake on our left and open fields of shooting stars and red maids on the right. Reaching the start of the

Two-Waters Trail, we start our 440-foot ascent to the Duna Vista Trail. The trail makes several switchbacks up the hill, then heads deep into the canyon above. The variety of wildflowers continues to increase as we continue up this trail. Once at the

Duna Vista Trail, you may take the right fork and descend 0.7 mile to Encinal Camp for a visit to the Lopez arm of the lake. Our trail turns left at this junction for a 0.5 mile hike along the ridge to the

Duna Vista Overlook. At the overlook, three benches make a good spot for a picnic lunch. Enjoy the views down the Arroyo Grande Valley out to the Oceano/Guadalupe Dunes. After lunch we retrace our steps to the

Duna Vista Alternate Route Trail. Turn right and follow this trail through lupine to another trail junction. The right fork heads up to the knoll ahead. Our trail uses the left fork, which descends down an old road to a meadow just above the lake. The trail continues to follow the old road further down toward the lake, then turns left to skirt the high water mark of the lake before reaching the

Duna Vista and Tuouski Trail. Retrace your steps for another 2.4 miles to get back to your car.

When the lake water level is low, you may cross the creek just past the pipeline, bypassing French Camp and shortening your trip by about half a mile.

CHORRO WILLOWS

FOSTER

SANTA LUCIA
MOUNTAINS

Hi Mountain

Usage:	Hikers, Horses, Mountain Bikes and Dogs on Leash.
Fee:	None
Distance:	1.4 Miles (One Way)
Elevation Gain/Loss:	+540/-240 Feet
Approx. Hiking Time:	2-3 Hours
Hike Rating:	Moderate
USGS Maps:	Tar Spring Ridge

Best Time to Hike: Winter, Spring, Late Fall

Point On Route:	Distance from Starting Point Miles(Km)	Elevation
Hi Mountain Trailhead	0.0 (0.0)	920
Switchback up hill	0.7 (1.1)	1060
Faint Trail Junction	1.0 (1.6)	1320
Ridge top	1.2 (2.0)	1460
Hi Mountain Road	1.4 (2.3)	1220

Directions to Trailhead: From Arroyo Grande, drive 2 miles east on Huasna Road. Bear left onto Lopez Drive, and drive 8 miles to Lopez Lake. Drive along the lake. After crossing the bridge just before Lopez Lake Entrance Station, turn right onto Hi Mountain Road (Arroyo Grande-Pozo Road), and drive 0.8 mile to Lopez Canyon Road. Continuing straight toward Pozo, drive 4.7 miles to the Hi Mountain Trailhead on the left. There is ample parking here.

Trail Overview: The Hi Mountain Trail was created upon the subdivision of Ranchita Estates. The old red farmhouse was the main headquarters of the original ranch. This short 1.4-mile trail wanders through a lush canyon, then climbs to a ridge top before descending to Hi Mountain Road. It provides a good staging area to the Los Padres National Forest for those on horseback. There are many private trails in the Ranchita Estates area. Please respect the rights of private property owners and stay on the public trail.

Trail Description:

Hi Mountain Trailhead. Our trail starts by passing through a gate heading into a cool canyon. A small stream is on our left. For the first ¾ mile we walk on a wide old road lush with vegetation and a variety of flowers all summer long. After the creek crossing, the trail comes to a junction marked by a sign pointing to the right, up a

steep switchback. The trail climbs sharply, then turns left to enter thick chaparral with views of a grassy hillside and oaks. Climbing almost 400 feet, we come to what might seem to be a

faint trail junction. Take the level trail to the right. The trail straight ahead leads onto private property. Climbing another short hill, we reach the ridge, which we follow a bit higher to the

ridge top. The ridge top offers spectacular views of Ranchita Estates and the Los Padres Forest to the north and east. On a clear day you might be able to see Caldwell Mesa far to the east, marked by a set of pine trees along a ridge top. We now continue east down a steep ridge to Hi Mountain Road. Be careful on this slippery part of the trail. Upon reaching

Hi Mountain Road, we suggest you make a right and follow the road 1.5 miles back to your starting point. This is a gentle walk past large oaks.

South County

Oceano Lagoon
Oso Flaco Lake

Oso Flaco Lake

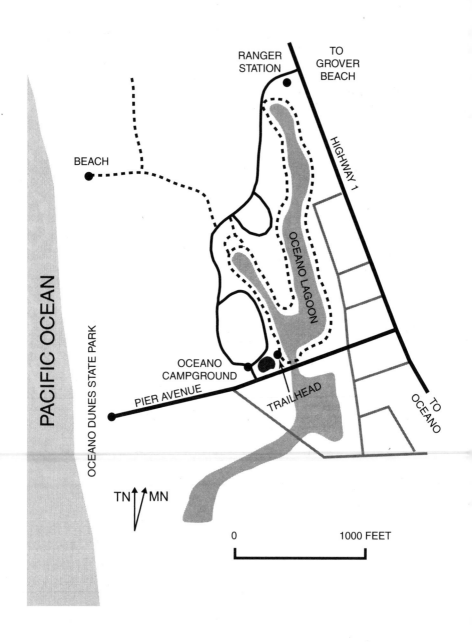

Oceano Lagoon

Guiton (Oceano Lagoon)

Usage:	Hikers Only
Fee:	None
Distance:	1.5-Mile Loop Trip
Elevation Gain/Loss:	0 feet
Approx. Hiking Time:	1 – 2 Hours
Hike Rating:	Easy
USGS Maps:	Oceano

Best Time to Hike: All Year

Directions to Trailhead: Take Highway 1 from Pismo Beach South. Cross Grand Avenue and continue approximately one mile to Pier Avenue. Drive 0.2 mile to the Oceano Campground, turn into the campground and park near the Visitor Center.

Trail Overview: Oceano Lagoon is a lush, tranquil spot with much to offer the visitor—birding, fishing and canoeing, as well as hiking. An abundance of Monterey pines, eucalyptus and willows makes this a cool refuge on a hot summer day. The trail itself is named after Harold E. Guiton, who donated five acres of lagoon property to California State Parks in the mid 1930's. A visitor center was built to educate the visitor on the natural resources of the area.

Trail Description:

Our trail starts east of the Visitor Center and goes north along the west side of the lagoon, on a partially paved path skirting the edge of the campground. Several spots here allow us to stop and observe wildlife. The trail winds around the north end of the lagoon, then heads south onto a peninsula before it turns north again. Reaching the north end of the lagoon, we come to a paved road leading to State Park Headquarters. Turn right on this road and cross a small bridge. The trail can be found just across the bridge. Turn right to traverse the east side of the lagoon. The forest is quite lush here. State Parks has built wooden bridges across the wettest areas of the trail. The trail ends at Pier Avenue, where a right turn and a walk along Pier Avenue takes us back to the Visitor Center parking lot.

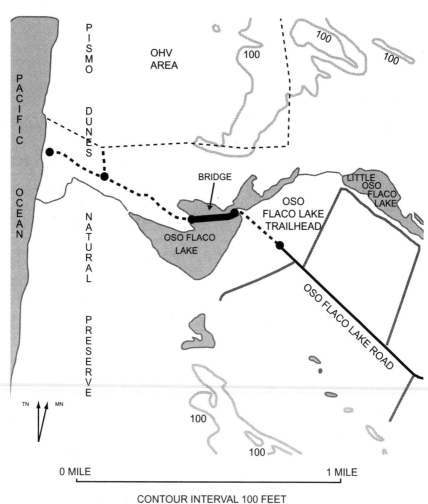

Oso Flaco Lake

Oso Flaco Lake

Usage:	Hikers, Wheel Chair Accessible
Fee:	$4 Parking Fee
Distance:	1 Mile
Elevation Gain/Loss:	+50/-50 Feet
Approx. Hiking Time:	1 – 2 Hours
Hike Rating:	Easy
USGS Maps:	Oceano

Best Time to Hike: All Year

Point On Route:	Distance from Starting Point Miles(Km)	Elevation
Oso Flaco Lake Trailhead	0.0 (0.0)	50
Bridge across Lake	0.2 (0.3)	50
End of Bridge	0.4 (0.6)	50
Junction	0.8 (1.9)	40
Pacific Ocean	1.0 (1.6)	0

Directions to Trailhead: From Highway 101 in Nipomo, take the Tefft Street exit and proceed 0.8 mile west to Orchard Road. Turn left, then drive 0.7 mile to Division Road. Turn right, then drive 3.2 miles to Oso Flaco Lake Road. Turn right onto this road and drive 5.3 miles to a parking lot at the end of the road. You will cross both Highway 1 and a set of railroad tracks before reaching the parking lot.

Oso Flaco Lake can also be reached from Highway 101. In Santa Maria, take the Main Street exit (Highway 166 West). Follow 166 to Highway 1 in Guadalupe. Turn north onto Highway 1. Drive through Guadalupe, then turn left onto Oso Flaco Lake Road. Drive to the end of the road and park in the parking lot.

Trail Overview: The 75-acre Oso Flaco (*Skinny Bear*) Lake is one of many fresh water lakes in the Guadalupe/Nipomo Dunes Preserve. To the north lies the Dune Lakes Preserve of seven fresh water lakes including Black Lake. The trail starts along an old road once used for access to the Pismo Dunes OHV area. It then crosses Oso Flaco Lake and continues out to the Pacific Ocean along an extensive boardwalk. Many plant and animal species can be found along this trail. For more adventure, head south across Oso Flaco

Creek and visit the dunes themselves, Coreopsis Hill, and Hidden Willow Valley. This area was once used by OHVs and has since been closed to this use. The Nature Conservancy undertook to restore the dunes to their original state, and the recovery process is well on its way. Management of Oso Flaco Lake is now handled by California State Parks.

This trail is wheelchair accessible.

Trail Description:

Oso Flaco Lake Trailhead. Our hike begins on the northwest end of the parking lot, along an old road with lush vegetation on both sides. A variety of wildflowers thrive along this paved portion of the path. At the end of the road you come to the long

bridge which crosses Oso Flaco Lake itself. There are many places to stop along the bridge for great views of the lake and the many bird species that thrive in this area. The small piles of scat on the bridge are evidence of how animals have adapted to human structures. The animals use it as a causeway. Reaching the

end of the bridge we enter the dune habitat. Many species of dune wildflowers, including Hookers primrose, can be found along this path. You might even see a red-legged frog warming in the sun. We soon come to a junction. The right path leads into the OHV recreation area. We continue straight a short distance, reaching the

Pacific Ocean. There are many places to enjoy on the beach, including Coreopsis Hill and Hidden Willow Valley.

References

Archaeological Evidence of Cultural Continuity from Chumash to Salinan Indians in California, by Mary Alice Baldwin. San Luis Obispo County Archaeological Society, 1972.

Audubon Society Field Guide of North American Trees, Western Region, by Elbert L. Little. Knopf, 1987.

Audubon Society Nature Guide of the Pacific Coast, by Bayard H. McConnaughey and Evelyn McConnaughey. Knopf, 1986.

Back Roads of the Central Coast, by Ron Stob. Bear Flag Books,1986.

California Insects, by Jerry A. Powell and Charles L. Hogue. University of California Press, 1979.

California's Changing Landscapes, by Gordon B. Oakeshott. McGraw-Hill, 1978.

Common Edible and Useful Plants of the West, by Muriel Sweet. Naturegraph Publishers, 1976.

Chumash, A Picture of Their World, by Bruce W. Miller. Sand River Press, 1988.

Dangerous Marine Animals of the Pacific Coast, by Christina Parsons. Helm Publishing, 1986.

Field Guide to the Gray Whale. Oceanic Society/Legacy, 1983.

Field Guide to Western Birds, by Roger Tory Peterson. Houghton Mifflin, 1972.

Geology of San Luis Obispo County, by David Chipping, from the author, 1987.

Guide to Western Wildlife, by Buddy Mays. Chronicle, 1977.

Jepson Manual, Higher Plants of California, by James C. Hickman, ed. University of California Press, 1993.

Lopez Guide: Trails, Plants, Wildlife, Geology, History, Fishing, by Robert Bodaracco. Department of General Services, County of San Luis Obispo, 1984.

Man and the California Condor, by Ian McMillan Dutton, 1968.

More Back Roads of the Central Coast, by Ron Stob. Bear Flag Books, 1989.

Morro Bay Meanderings, by Harold Wieman. (2nd Edition) Bear Flag Books, 1984.

Nature Walks on the San Luis Coast, by Harold Wieman. Bear Flag Books, 1980.

Pacific Coast Inshore Fishes, by Daniel W. Gotshall. Sea Challengers, 1981.

The Painted Rock, by Myron Angel. Bear Flag Books, 1910,1979.

San Luis Obispo County Pathways: A Guide to the Historical Highlights of the County, by Loren Nicholson. New Paradigm Press, 1981.

The Vascular Plants of San Luis Obispo County, California, by Robert F. Hoover. University of California Press, 1970.

The Vascular Plants of San Luis Obispo County, California, Color Supplement, by Robert F. Hoover. Betty L. Hoover, 1974.

Uncommon Guide to San Luis Obispo County, California, by Lachlan P. MacDonald. Bear Flag Books, 1989.

Vignettes of History in San Luis Obispo County, by Louisiana Clayton Dart. Mission Federal Savings, 1978.

Wildflowers of the West, by Mabel Crittenden and Dorothy Telfer. Celestial Arts, 1975.

Index